JOHN DEWEY
AND THE EXPERIMENTAL SPIRIT IN PHILOSOPHY

JOHN DEWEY

AND THE EXPERIMENTAL SPIRIT
IN PHILOSOPHY

Four Lectures Delivered at Yale University
Commemorating the 100th Anniversary of the
Birth of John Dewey

EDITED BY CHARLES W. HENDEL

THE LIBERAL ARTS PRESS

NEW YORK

PREFACE

Four lectures were presented at Yale University on March 6, 9, 11, and 13, 1959, in commemoration of the one hundredth anniversary of the birth of John Dewey. By way of preface the opening lecture recalled that Dewey had delivered the Terry Lectures for 1933, *A Common Faith*. Eighteen years later Dewey again visited the University, invited for the celebration of the 250th Anniversary, and he was chosen as the representative philosopher in a galaxy of distinguished persons on whom Yale had been proud to confer its honorary degree. It was thus in order that the four of us, who are members of the department of philosophy, should design our series of lectures with the aim of honoring a great achievement.

We make no pretension to be doing full justice to the lifework of John Dewey. We have treated only certain aspects of it and ventured no comprehensive statement or evaluation of his philosophy. Our intention has simply been to present certain insights found in his writings of which we ourselves have high appreciation and which we believe to be of present-day, and indeed enduring, significance.

We proceeded empirically to discover our common theme indicated in the title. Each one chose to write on what he deemed a topic of prime importance and when all of us had developed our several themes we met in conference to find out if, perchance, some ruling idea were governing our thoughts. It turned out, then, that

our lectures on Dewey in one way or another constituted a testament to philosophy practiced in the experimental spirit.

The original texts of the lectures have been slightly
revised for publication. Omissions that had to be made
on the occasion of their delivery were restored. Some
amplifications have been supplied for completeness of
statement for the reader. There has also been documen-
tation of quotations and references.

We are grateful for the interest of Mr. Oskar Piest,
Editor of the Liberal Arts Press, who urged publication
and made every effort to see that the lectures would actually appear in print during the commemorative year
itself.

CHARLES W. HENDEL

July 1, 1959

CONTENTS

THE NEW EMPIRICISM AND THE
PHILOSOPHICAL TRADITION

By Charles W. Hendel

1859—The Times and the Man

THESE LECTURES are in commemoration of the hundredth anniversary of the birth of John Dewey in 1859. Commemoration is a particularly appropriate word: it evokes the image of many things remembered together. Many important things did happen in that year 1859, things of great consequence which we should first recall.

Darwin published the *Origin of Species*. The difference that work has since made in the outlook and general thinking of men is so great that it stands out now as a permanent landmark in the general education of the western world. Its significance is far more than its immediate role of priming the biological sciences for their tremendous advance since that day. The idea of evolution has effected vast changes throughout the whole realm of human experience.

Many years of searching for conclusive evidence had preceded Darwin's publication of the evolutionary hypothesis, but we may also remember that the initial resistance to it was so great that something like twenty years were required, too, for its acceptance as a valid theory. It was during these years that John Dewey grew to manhood and received his own personal education. His college years were spent at the University of Vermont in his home city of Burlington. The formal curriculum consisted of the required courses, Greek, Latin, ancient history, analytic geometry, and calculus. Besides these subjects he studied geology in Dana's text, and physiology in another text by T. H. Huxley. More important than those textbooks may have been the symposia and current articles in several English periodicals available in the College library, the *Fortnightly Review*, the *Contemporary Review*, and the *Nineteenth Century*, where Huxley and others debated evolution.[1] Their argument about the theory of evolution could not be confined to the scientific interchanges in learned journals for it was too controversial. It provoked anew the so-called "conflict of science with religion." Those vigorous disputations of the day conducted in the journals of opinion were a very proper nutriment for philosophers like John Dewey and Henri Bergson, another contemporary, also born in 1859. Years afterward, on the fiftieth anniversary of the *Origin of Species*, Dewey remembered Darwin and honored the occasion with a commemorative essay, *The Influence of Darwin on Modern Philosophy*.

But the idea of evolution was not all that caught the attention of such young, alert minds alive to the doings of their time. There were publications relating also to the realm of action—to politics, society, and world history. The year 1859 saw the appearance of John Stuart

[1] These and the following biographical details are cited from "Biography of John Dewey," edited by Jane M. Dewey in *The Philosophy of John Dewey*, "The Library of Living Philosophers," edited by Paul Arthur Schilpp (Evanston and Chicago, 1939).

Mill's *Essay on Liberty*. Was there anything revolutionary or of great consequence about that essay? The battle
for liberty, was it not securely won? Mill seemed to say
so himself in the opening lines of his chapter on "the
liberty of thought and expression": "The time, it is to
be hoped, is gone by when any defense would be necessary of the liberty of the press." An American reader
might reflect complacently that this was a right already
secured in the Constitution. Yet that great observer De
Tocqueville (and he, too, should receive mention now,
inasmuch as he died in that memorable year 1859)
had flown some danger signals about "democracy in
America." And as one reads on in Mill's *Essay* his own
words were by no means reassuring, for he had only
written cautiously, "it is to be hoped," and then went
on to make quite despairing observations about the
trends of social life, the threats due to mass opinion,
its prejudices, "intolerance," "dead dogma," pressures
"wearing [men and women] down into uniformity,"
forcing "conformity,"—and he saw the dire prospect of
"the sacrifice of the entire moral courage of the human
mind," and of "individuality," and of the will to make
"new and original experiments in living." This is not
Dewey speaking, but Mill; yet who could tell the difference? [2] They were the selfsame words, pointing to identical evils, and betraying the same concern about social
tyrannies over the individual, the threats to liberty of
mind and the right to creative experiment. Dewey very
early learned the lesson that democracy is a problem,

[2] See Dewey's references to J. S. Mill in "An Empirical Survey
of Empiricisms," *Studies in The History of Ideas* (New York,
1935), III, 18 ff.

or a task to be performed, not a matter about which Americans could rest complacent. And hard thinking was necessary to reach practical solutions.

But in 1859 another publication of quite opposite meaning had also come out and it was gaining some attention, too, during Dewey's formative years. This was Karl Marx's *Critique of Political Economy,* critical of the doctrine of Mill's earlier *Principles of Political Economy* (1848), and critical, too, of the whole doctrine of classical liberalism. Here was another commentary on contemporary civilization. Its appearance was symptomatic of a wide-spreading consciousness of the human consequences of the industrial revolution. That the "revolution" actually amounted to a social and moral revolution Marx was driving home with a vigor and self-assurance that had been lacking in liberalism and in the more polite forms of socialism. The new socialism would be scientific, not Utopian, and just as scientific, its protagonists claimed, as the new Darwinism. It would be very practical, too, indicating a line of action, for it was a philosophy with a program. In the Preface to his *Critique* Marx announced the new theory: "In the social production of their subsistence men enter into determined and necessary relations with each other which are independent of their wills." We have called it "theory." For Marx and Engels this declaration was not at all theoretical—it simply stated the fact. Here was the plain, realistic law of all human existence, the law of material necessity, the dialectic of logic in human history that overrules individual lives and determines all the institutions of society and the whole of human culture. The freedom of man? That consisted simply in

men's understanding the historical stage of the movement of collective destiny and then assuming the particular role that fell to them as individuals, some to
march forward in the vanguard—those with the fullest
knowledge of realities—leading the rest who follow and
who in so doing enter into the common inheritance of a
better life.

The sense of all this was the very opposite of Mill's
careful argument for liberty and individualism. And
Dewey would not take kindly to that philosophy and its
logic, so-called, of a materially deterministic dialectic.
Like Charles Peirce and William James, he reacted
strongly against the idea of "iron necessity" in the realm
of life and history, and he delivered his own attack on
it later under the title, "The Superstition of Necessity." [3] Yet something remained from that scarifying
portraiture by Marx of the condition of man in an industrial society. Prophecy aside, the social facts indeed
were not to be ignored. They were the same sort of facts
that Dewey had encountered in the essays of Frederic
Harrison in the *Fortnightly Review* and in Auguste
Comte's *Positive Philosophy* as rendered in concise
form by Harriet Martineau. The common burden of
the various writings was "the disorganization of existing social life." [4] And whether or not the young Dewey
felt disposed toward political socialism he would certainly—to judge from the sequel—not be unmoved by
the evidence of such careless, ruthless, ungoverned in-

[3] The "Monist," summarized in the *Philosophical Review,* July,
1893, II, 488 f.
[4] See the *Philosophy of John Dewey,* "Library of Living Philosophers," p. 12.

dividualism as disclosed by those various writers. Some social control was plainly needed. But in a democracy this comes best through education, especially education in personal responsibility. Here the proper task of philosophy was early revealed to be, as expressed later in the *Essays in Experimental Logic* (1916), "to enforce the sense of a social calling and responsibility." [5] And Dewey subsequently declared in *Experience and Nature* (1925): "Philosophy should terminate in an art of social control." [6] This is the mature position of the man who as a youth had to find his way between an individualism and a collectivism, and tentatively, as an experimental philosopher ought to proceed.

One more reference is necessary to this early time of prime influences. Dewey decided, upon graduating in 1879 when he was hardly twenty, that he wanted to teach and become a professional philosopher. He had already learned something of the craft. His own teachers had introduced him to the works of some great masters —notably the *Republic* of Plato, and the writings of English Empiricism. One teacher, Rev. Prof. James Marsh, who was speculatively inclined, had been attracted to the German idealistic philosophers, by way of Coleridge—and indeed Coleridge, Dewey is reported to have said, remained one of his own favorite authors. But it was not until Dewey had two years of experience in high schools elsewhere and had returned to Burlington to teach in a neighboring village school at Charlotte that he knew surely what he wanted to do. Then his erstwhile professor, H. A. P. Torrey, went on walks with

[5] *Op. cit.,* p. 72.
[6] *Op. cit.,* p. 127.

him confiding to him his own deep interest in Hegel, an interest which he had developed through reading the only philosophical periodical then published in America, the *Journal of Speculative Philosophy*. This was edited by W. T. Harris, a former superintendent of schools in St. Louis, who had come to know of Hegel through some German exiles of the 1848 exodus. Dewey became so interested in Hegel and philosophy that he mailed an essay to Harris asking him to judge it, and virtually asking him to answer this question: "Can I be a philosopher?" The oracle apparently said "Yes," and so it came to pass that Dewey traveled to Johns Hopkins in 1882, on borrowed money, to begin graduate study and his professional career.

Further details of biography we must eschew, and attend henceforth only to the philosophy. However, a moment's further lingering is warranted simply to note the fact of that grateful relationship of Dewey with Harris, and indirectly with the *Journal of Speculative Philosophy*. The *Journal* was then the first forum of philosophical expression in the United States. To it the new men of America, the classics-to-be, were sending their first speculative adventures of thought. For example, an article had appeared in 1878 entitled "Remarks on Spencer's Definition of Mind as Correspondence," by one listed in the table of contents as "Dr. W. James." We can readily imagine in that signature, "Dr.," a certain pride of the young laureate William James. The article contained the same kind of attack on Spencer as Henri Bergson in France was then making on the accepted notion of the "adaptation" of the organism to environment which uncritically assumed a materialistic determinism. Dewey himself had expressed like objections, and in fact his own very first publishing venture was an article in the *Journal* in 1882 entitled: "The Metaphysical Assumptions of Materialism." So our story begins in the climate of Hegel, and with the philosophical spirit of criticism.

In coming to know Hegel through teachers of philosophy toward whom he felt grateful ever after, Dewey approached with favorable prepossessions a great master of the philosophical tradition. For Hegel's marvelous gift of imagination had enabled him to identify the living concerns of men in their own particular times and places in history and to appreciate their relevant problems and solutions, and he had recounted in grand style and with apposite detail the vicissitudes of philosophy as it advances from insight to insight through the great historic ordeal of argument. That sympathetic introduction which Dewey had to Hegel must have introduced at the same time something of all this varied history of philosophy into his own experience. His friend William James later discerned how very much Dewey owed to Hegel when he said: "You come from Hegel; I come from empiricism." This Dewey himself was perfectly willing to acknowledge, as when he wrote, "Acquaintance with Hegel has left a permanent deposit in my thinking. . . . I still should believe that there is greater richness and greater variety of insight in Hegel than in any other systematic philosopher." [7]

Of course that tribute to Hegel does not place Dewey in the ranks of the opposition to empiricism. What James said was true enough—you come from Hegel. Yet

[7] *Contemporary American Philosophy,* II, 21.

Dewey could properly have added, "and I have arrived at a new type of empiricism." [8] This is our theme; or, more precisely, empiricism in the "experimental spirit."

I. *Critique of the Philosophical Tradition*

But now we wonder: how is it possible to come from insights of Hegel to empiricism? The question is very natural and proper when one thinks back on the many occasions when John Dewey attacked all "philosophical tradition." Indeed, his writings abound in criticisms of all things "traditional." The adjective is invariably a derogatory epithet. And was not the philosophy of Hegel the "classic" example of the "tradition" of philosophy? We must consider then, before proceeding further with the question of his relation to Hegel, Dewey's very critical attitude toward tradition. And at once one learns to appreciate the careful and tentative or "experimental habit" of Dewey's own thinking.

True, there is much disparaging criticism of traditional things throughout his writings. On the other hand, he speaks sometimes in praise of "tradition," and especially he values the "continuity" and "sequence of tradition" which, he avers, is "a necessity of intelligent thought and action." [9] What really provoked his prevailing mood of disparagement were the "congerers," as William James would have called them, of traditional

[8] "An Empirical Survey of Empiricisms," p. 22.

[9] "The Significance of the Problem of Knowledge" (1897) in *The Influence of Darwin on Philosophy and Other Essays in Contemporary Thought* (New York, 1910), p. 293. See also John Herman Randall, Jr., *Nature and Historical Experience* (New York, 1958), p. 2.

thinking—"the domination exercised by prejudice, narrow interest, routine custom and the authority which
issues from institutions"; "the force of tradition and
dogmatic authority"; [10] "stale repetition and blind acceptance of authority"; "influential forms of supersti-
tious dogmatism and arbitrary political authority." [11]
All such tirades against evils, of course, recall the words
of Mill. The desiderata, too, are obvious; a sheer rid-
dance of all that blind influence, prejudice, routine, authority, and orthodoxy, and then the liberation of intelligence to "fresh, unhampered personal experience." [12]
The goal of free philosophy is to recover "the genuinely
creative effort of the individual," [13] and in particular
the active, creative "office" of reason.[14] Is not this last
thought in the pure Hegelian strain?

There are in truth quite antithetical attitudes in
Dewey regarding tradition, with the negative attitude,
as already remarked, far more in evidence and prepon-
derant.[15] He pressed his charges against the evils per-
sistently, even relentlessly. But even this proves most il-
luminating when it is critically examined. Why, we ask,
that lifelong stance of opposition to the traditional?
Was there no lesson for him in the *Logic* of Hegel that

[10] *The Quest for Certainty* (New York, 1929), last chapter, pp.
311-12.

[11] *An Empirical Survey*, pp. 12, 16.

[12] *Ibid.*, p. 16.

[13] *Experience and Nature*, p. 240.

[14] Later, Dewey preferred the expressions, the "function" of
"creative intelligence."

[15] See the opening of "A Recovery of Philosophy" in *Creative
Intelligence* (New York, 1917), pp. 1-7.

the mind must move on from the negative moment of antithesis (here the antitraditionalist thesis) to a transcending synthesis? Of course he knew that doctrine very well, and though he rejected its metaphysical dialectic he incorporated an "insight" from it into his own *Logic,* as when he wrote: "Nothing is more important than the institution of contradictory propositions." Their value or importance consists in their being instrumental to something beyond themselves, for the negative is an essential stage among the "stages of progress in the conduct of inquiry," within "the continuum of experiential inquiry." [16] The goal of the affair, Dewey then added in the very words of the last paragraph of the *Logic,* is to obtain and be able to utilize "stable beliefs." But then why in this particular instance of his own opinion about tradition did he seem to stay so fixed in the extreme and negative groove?

Those primary moral concerns of John Dewey which we noted at the outset must be remembered here if we are to understand that prevalent antitraditionalist set of his mind. It is precisely the attitude of a person who demands corrective action. It is characteristic of the moralist. Thus Rousseau, for instance, continued in like manner with his own early radical condemnation of traditional civilization unabated through his later constructive writings on education, government, and society. He never ceased rubbing in with all the eloquence he could muster how absolutely shocking the contrast is between the right order of life and the es-

[16] *Logic: Theory of Inquiry* (New York, 1938), pp. 197, 309, 534.

tablished order. Kant likewise maintained an absolute distinction in this life between the ethical "ought" and the prevalent practice. Plato, who insisted on the shocking chasm between the Ideal and the actual, may be included, too. This habit of dwelling protractedly on the intolerable evils of the present even while delineating the ideal possibilities of the right and good is motivated by a strongly practical and ethical concern. An unmitigating exposure of evils *incites* men to act. It works even though they are told in the same breath that they can never attain but only approximate to the Good Life or to the perfect society of a Republic.

Dwelling everlastingly on the negative is thus the moralist's way of summoning the energies of men to effect great needed changes. Dewey himself avows this, implicitly at least, when in criticising both Hegel and Bergson he associates his own philosophy with "a call to effort." [17] It is the moralist in Dewey, consequently, which makes him refuse the famous Hegelian proposition that the real is the rational and the rational the real. He was dead-set against any soothing reconcilement of the ideal and actual, done in the mere words of a philosophy. No solution by wholesale formula will do the trick. A transcending synthesis, seemingly assured by logic, when published to the world may appear to others to solve everything, thus lulling their minds into another dogmatic slumber. The labor of the negative must be each man's own labor, not something to look at as a spectator of the grand procession of a victorious Spirit.

[17] *Experience and Nature*, p. 51.

We can see in this very demand for personal action an example of "the pervasiveness of tradition" [18] in Dewey's own thinking. For there is apparent in it precisely the spirit of the modern individualistic and revolutionary tradition as previously expressed by Rousseau and Kant. Indeed Dewey actually appropriates the magnificent phrase "the Copernican Revolution" from Kant. But again he takes his own stand, for it is not a case with him of "back to Kant."

The closing chapter of the *Quest for Certainty* was entitled "The Copernican Revolution." It outlines a new "philosophical revolution," and distinguishes it from Kant's "alleged revolution" which only "consisted in making explicit what was implicit in the classic tradition." [19] The revolutionary view which Kant had proposed to set philosophy on a firm basis and an assured course of progress comparable with that of modern science was nothing else than a turnabout in theory where knowledge was still conceived only as a relation between thought and things. Everything that transpired in consequence was still confined to an intellectual circle of experience. Kant had there been a victim of "the intellectualist fallacy" [20] as had many others before him moving in the dominant philosophical tradition. A genuinely revolutionary hypothesis must have conse-

[18] *Creative Intelligence,* "A Recovery of Philosophy" (1917), p. 54. The explicit reference in the text was to Bergson.

[19] *Op. cit.,* p. 287.

[20] *Quest.,* p. 291. The phrase "the intellectualist fallacy" had been used by Graham Wallas in *Human Nature and Politics* (1908), cited by Currin V. Shields in his Introduction to James Mill's *An Essay in Government* (New York, 1958), p. 25.

quences manifested in the whole ambit of human experience. It will modify not only our understanding of
science and how man achieves science (which Kant had
shown, as we shall see later), but also our understanding of human conduct and the relations of the ideal and
actual and how men attain to the appropriate values of
life in the course of living under the institutions of
their society. According to the new, present-day Copernican hypothesis, knowledge and action are more or-
ganically, more intimately and essentially related than
had been conceived by Kant or even by Hegel, both of
whom had celebrated in their own way the active, creative office of reason. Dewey's work is thus a long-drawn-
out critique of the philosophical tradition for its failure to understand the right use of reason and its essentially practical role.[21] The revolution was not to be
accomplished at one stroke or by a single turn of the
screw, reversing an old order. It required many essays
by many men working at their unavoidable common
problems in many situations and making trial of their
ideas for solutions. The inherent modesty of Dewey ob-
scures the significance of his own "essays" not only in
experimental logic but over a vast range of questions.
After what would be regarded by any other man as a
long lifetime of work, all he claimed for himself at the
age of seventy was, in the last words of his chapter on
the "Copernican Revolution," that he had so far merely
"tried to indicate in outline the nature of the task to be
accomplished." [22]

[21] See "A Recovery of Philosophy" in *Creative Intelligence*, pp.
27 f.
[22] *Op. cit.*, p. 313.

What of "traditional" empiricism? [23] Throughout Dewey's writings it, too, is subjected to a critique. The "orthodox British empiricism" was a doctrine with serious flaws. One was the uncritical assumption that there are primitive elements—elements of knowledge in the form of psychological entities or sense data—given immediately in perception, whereas these are really sophisticated products of reflection and experimental inquiry.[24] Another fault was the empiricist "contempt for general ideas," ignoring the truth that "theorizing emancipates experience." There is also failure to recognize the "necessity of abstract hypothesis," and to discern the "value inherent even in the most subjective reflection." [25] Convicting the traditional empiricism of such grave faults, Dewey indignantly protested at its near "monopoly," as he called it, of the worthy term "empiricism." [26]

In these criticisms Dewey has made use of insights of both Kant and Hegel regarding the role of ideas and reason in handling the data of sensuous intuition or perception. His attitude toward the traditional empiricism is disparaging, even iconoclastic, as much as to say that it is well left thoroughly demolished by its critics. Indeed, what he himself valued in the British tradition of philosophy was precisely such an antitraditional spirit. As he said in his *Empirical Survey of Em-*

[23] See "A Recovery of Philosophy" in *Creative Intelligence,* pp. 6-15, 23.

[24] See *Essays in Experimental Logic,* Introduction, dated 1916, p. 25.

[25] The citations are, in order, from *Essays,* pp. 25 and 439; from *Logic,* p. 519; and again *Essays,* pp. 196-7.

[26] *Experience and Nature* (First Edition), p. 4.

piricisms (1935): "The important thing, to my mind, in this empirical movement was its critical negative side . . . as a dissolvent of tradition and doctrine." [27] Yet it had, besides, one enduring positive merit, namely, that it referred always to "fresh unhampered personal experience." [28]

Now this last phrase inevitably recalls Hegel's own characterization of empiricism in the "Logic" of the *Encyclopedia of the Philosophical Sciences:* "The lesson of empiricism is that man must see for himself and feel that he is present in every fact of knowledge which he is to accept." [29] Empiricism is thus represented as the quest for authentic, personal, self-won knowledge. But this may also be said of the entire philosophical tradition from Descartes and Bacon onward. It is the phenomenon to which Whitehead has referred as "the subjective principle" of modern philosophy.

But this broad characterization of empiricism could well be a source of liberation from the traditional empiricism. It revealed the possibility of a "new type of empiricism."

II. *The New Empiricism*

The distinctive features of the new empiricism should be sought for in those writings where the thought of Dewey seems at once most originative and most significant.

[27] *Op. cit.,* p. 18.
[28] *Ibid.,* p. 16.
[29] *Op. cit.,* chap. iv, sect. 38, translation by William Wallace (Oxford, 1892), p. 78.

A beginning of the trail from Hegel to the new empiricism is discernible in a study of psychology published as "The Reflex Arc in Psychology." [30] Dewey modestly proposed his essay as if it were merely a footnote to the previous work of William James on the subject. Dewey here reveals his own individual power as a thinker. As we review this piece of original work and the others that follow, it should be remembered that Dewey himself pursued his vision—and he does say himself, "philosophy is vision, imagination, reflection" [31]— while finding his way amidst the confusing traditional underbrush. In his psychological study he was working upon the age-long problem of perception, but envisaging it in a new fundamental way, in liaison with action. Here he utilized the insights of William James and—as we shall see—something from Hegel. But it was essentially his own achievement, the fruit of a "genuinely creative effort of the individual," [32] to apply in this case language which Dewey used in other connections.

The reflex arc had been described as a process initiated by a definite stimulus which affects the sense organs and provokes a motor response toward an outside object of which the stimulus is a mere advance notice. The in-between, the central phase, could at times be very elaborate, an interval occupied by the thinking processes necessary to gain clearance for the appropriate impulse. This accepted story of the process seemed, however, shot with an artificial discontinuity. The rule is that nothing happens without first a stimulus from

[30] *Psychological Review,* 1896.
[31] "A Recovery of Philosophy," *Creative Intelligence,* p. 65.
[32] *Experience and Nature,* p. 240.

the sensory side. Each time the circuit must begin with
sensation and it ends in a motor reaction. Then there is
a blank until something external starts up another
process. The mechanism, so to speak, is not conceived to
start at any other phase. Nor can the later consequences
have any bearing on the meaning of the original phenomenon. Nothing ever happens to the perception of
that which affords the stimulus, that is, to our apprehension of its meaning in the light of what ensues upon
it. But this is, after all, a strange reading of experience.
For experience is here represented simply as an unre-
lated series of arcs. But William James himself had previously described in his *Principles of Psychology* and
the famous chapter on the "Stream of Thought" the
"continuity of experience" and portrayed the "stream
of consciousness" with its "transitive" and "substantive"
states in a continuing functional relation with each
other.

Dewey's own genius lay in taking seriously the organic continuity of the whole performance. The changes
in the complexion of our experience may proceed sometimes from the sensory side, sometimes from motor
action, simply depending on the conditions. The responses reveal the meaning of the stimulus and define
the attributes of the object from which it comes. So
there is one continuous round of activity and percep-
tivity, with no one thing always first or always final. In
every instance what starts things going is some "conflict" between these "members" of "a whole act." A certain prior "co-ordination" is broken by some internal
incompatibility which may be occasioned not only by
happenings without, but also by inner purposes press-

ing for satisfaction and denied. According to this new concept, then, experience tends to be integral but suffers on occasion a partial "phase" of disintegration through some lack of accord or mutual "adaptation" of the motor dispositions and the perceptive factors. This organic logic of the circuit may be regarded, perhaps, as the paradigm for Dewey's subsequent philosophy: the "whole act" and the "members" therein are mutually defined by their functions in respect to each other within the process of life.

Another concept could have been employed in the analysis instead of the reflex arc concept, namely, that of "system." It would then be apparent how profoundly the ideas of Hegel worked within the developing originality of John Dewey. Further recollections of Hegel come to mind, such characteristic phrases as these: "the truth is the whole"; "the theoretical is essentially contained in the practical." [33] Opposition or conflict, the negative factor, is essential to advance in knowledge and life, in society and in history. Experience is always dialectical, not by any means a logic of thought alone but of all the phenomena of existence. By Dewey's own testimony such insights lasted long in his thinking. Late in his career we find the homage to Hegel in the very language of such a phrase as: "Every instance of dialectic is itself existential." [34]

Be that as it may, it seems that the first lesson of the new empiricism was this—there is an essential intercalation of thinking and acting in experience and in all

[33] *The Philosophy of Right,* translated by T. M. Knox (Oxford, 1945), p. 227.
[34] *Experience and Nature,* p. 287.

knowledge. This was what the philosophers of the tradition—empiricists as well as rationalists—had never learned. It was in view of this and its philosophical sequel that a new Copernican revolution would be ultimately announced.

Meanwhile the advance toward the new empiricism was slow and tentative, requiring many "essays." The year immediately following the publication of the "Reflex Arc Concept" Dewey wrote an essay on "The Problem of Knowledge" (1897), where he passed in review the whole course of modern philosophy. He stressed therein, as Hegel had done, the personal or subjective dimension of experience. Two years later came another essay entitled *Consciousness and Experience* (1899), where he actually avowed, "there is something in experience, something in things which the physical and biological sciences do not touch. . . . It is psychology which tells us how this possible experience [of scientific fact] loses its barely hypothetical character, and is stamped with categorical unquestioned experiencedness, how, in a word, it becomes here and now in some uniquely individualized life." [35] In 1903 he first presented his *Essays on Experimental Logic,* reissued in 1916. At that later date he had qualms about all these early essays so that he appended a long note to the one on *Consciousness and Experience,* the burden of which is the same as his attempted correction in the new (1916) Introduction to

[35] The two essays mentioned were republished in *The Influence of Darwin on Philosophy* (New York, 1910), and the quotation is from p. 269.

the *Essays,* where he confessed a fear that his thought
then was "infected by the subjectivism of the positions
against which it was directed." [36] Yet he would not sur-
render the term "experience" merely because of that
liability. He insisted on it because it was the only word
that could convey "the actual focussing of the world at
one point on a focus of immediate shining appar-
ency." [37] And even in the late *Experience and Nature*
(1925), he stuck to his guns: "Experience denotes 'what
is experienced,' the world of events and persons; and it
denotes that world caught up into experiencing the career and destiny of mankind." [38] And as to the "experiencing," the "what is experienced" must be present as
"something enjoyed or suffered, had and used, in conscious experience." [39] Echoes still of Hegel's words on
empiricism, "man must see for himself and feel that he
is present in every fact of knowledge which he is to accept."

The essay of 1906, *Experience and Objective Idealism,* seems to have been critical. The struggle with subjectivism had culminated in a problematic situation,
precisely the kind of thing which, according to his own
theory, is the growing point of knowledge and experience. The essay opened on a problematic note: "Idealism as a philosophic system stands in such a delicate relation to experience. . . ." [40] Dewey then appears to be
headed away from objective idealism and toward what

[36] *Essays,* p. 26.
[37] *Ibid.,* pp. 7, 61, 71.
[38] *Op. cit.,* p. 28.
[39] *Ibid.,* p. 110.
[40] *The Influence of Darwin,* p. 198.

we might call an "objective" empiricism. For at this point comes the second lesson of empiricism, one which Dewey learned from Charles Peirce and William James. He pays his tribute to them together in this very essay.

Peirce states his concept of "experience" as "that which is forced upon a man's recognition will-he, nill-he, and shapes his thoughts to something quite different from what they naturally would have taken." And Peirce adds that this meaning should be accepted "as a landmark which it would be a crime to disturb or displace." And James had described experience, in the chapter on "Necessary Truths" in his *Psychology*, as "the foreign element that forces the hand of thought and controls its efficacy"—all of which, Dewey remarks, "goes back to Locke." [41]

It had been characteristic of Locke, as well as of Bacon before him, to stress that experience is of particulars, and Dewey himself had already written in *The Postulate of Immediate Empiricism* (1905): "Experience is always of *thats* . . ."; [42] a position retained in the opening of *Experience and Nature:* "Denotation comes first and last." But in between first and last a process goes on which is essential and more important than the particulars. It is here, in respect to this process, that Dewey developed his own characteristic form of empiricism.

[41] Peirce in *Monist*, XVI, 150; James, *Psychology*, II, 618, quoted by Dewey in his essay, "Experience and Objective Idealism," in *Influence of Darwin*, p. 202; Locke, *Essay*, Bk. II, ch. II, sect. 2.

[42] In *Influence of Darwin*, p. 237.

Consider how experience "forces the recognition" of something "foreign" to thought, or how fact can "control" thought. A typical answer had been that it is the sheer "force" or "vivacity" of the particulars given in sensation. Now it is true that such things as sensations apparently force themselves upon our notice so that they cannot be ignored. But the inability to ignore them is not the same thing as "recognition" of what is foreign. The impression does intimate the presence of something in particular, but precisely *what* it is remains to be determined. Hegel's "insight" was pertinent, that a process of "making determinate" is involved, nay, a whole elaborate sequence of determinations as to the fact and truth of perception and that this is a continuing theoretical business in conjunction with the information from perception. However, the earlier exponents of empiricism made a quite separate point relevant to the question. "We must bring men to particulars, *and their regular series and order*," Bacon had written in *Novum Organum* (XXXVI).[43] Locke, too, treated "the constant and regular succession of ideas in a waking man" as "the measure and standard of all other successions." (Bk. II, ch. XIV) Hume further analyzed experience into the "constant conjunction" of objects of one species with those of another species—and experience in this form is the only warrant for the operations of the mind in causal inferences, affording a knowledge of "matter of fact and existence." It is this regular and constant *order* of the particulars that forces our recognition of fact, shapes our sequence of thought, corrects our vagaries, and makes possible the control of specula-

[43] Italics mine.

tion. It is this insistent "having things in just such unique, irreparable and compelling ways," as Dewey says, that conveys to us that sense of "the foreign element." [44]

Incidentally, what Hume had said about this order is especially worth noting, for it is prophetic: whatever is "constant" and "regular" Hume envisaged as "natural." The order of particulars is Nature's order and control that regulates our beliefs, corrects or verifies them. It is nature "that determines us" to think thus and so—thus the phrase ran. Hume's own keen surmise here was the precursor of a coming phase of "naturalism."

But we are not yet finished with Locke, for Dewey's own frequent recourse to him requires one more look at this passage on natural knowledge: "Experience is that which in this part we must depend on. And it were to be wished that it were more improved." [45] Now the "improvement of the understanding" had been the concern of Descartes before, as well as of his own contemporary, Spinoza, each of whom had proffered a "method" for it. However, this method applied to the examination of the mind itself, seeking the improvement in an internal clarification there. But the empirical philosophers leaned the other way, toward external things and transactions with them, and proposed their "experimental" method for the regulation of the mind. This, in the philosophy of Locke, was still very much an ideal, a guiding star, remote and not yet steadily followed. The theory was too conservative and not boldly enough developed.

[44] *Experience and Nature,* p. 19.
[45] *Essay Concerning Human Understanding,* Bk. IV, ch. III.

"For the most part," the "mind is passive," said Locke, speaking of the very first "act of sensation," and this largely passive aspect tends to dominate his account of knowledge from experience. Hume indeed had been interested in the "operations" of the understanding, but even in his account we simply "find" that events occur in certain regular constant conjunctions and we assume their order as rules of our experience valid for the future, and always. The whole point of a radically "experimental" logic, however, would be that really to improve knowledge one must deliberately experiment. And the business of an experiment is not merely adding more items to an already accepted collection of facts but reconstruing anew all of them. Experiment thus becomes the growing point of the body of knowledge.

Now, although Dewey objected to Kant's lending so much authority to a later subjectivist notion that everything depends on mind—Kant's phrase "the mind *makes* Nature" having had most unfortunate consequences in history—nonetheless Kant was the great enlightener on this question of the precise role of experiment. However mistaken he had been in supposing that he could ever deduce a complete and final system of categories for the understanding of appearances in space and time, it was surely a tremendous advance for empirical philosophy when in his Preface to the second edition of the *Critique of Pure Reason* he took the actual scientific procedure of Galileo, Torricelli, and Stahl as his model and showed that one only gains knowledge when advancing first a constructive idea of the possible solution of a problem and then experimenting accordingly, eliciting from Nature the precise answers to the questions posed. The concept *a priori* really has there an essential role. Forming concepts and theorizing constitute indispensable factors in experimentation, and consequently in all knowledge. The fault with Kant, then, had been his rationalistic claim to establish once and for all a timeless, complete scheme of forms for whatever may happen in time to come. But the Kantian view of the *lead* that must be taken by human intelligence and of the *a priori* function of rational concepts deepened and transformed both the theory of knowledge and the modern view of experience. Dewey for his own part insisted that what Kant had called the "spontaneity" of mind must be exerted on all individual occasions, both in the discovering of the relevant useful categories and in the construction of the experiment through which one tests the hypothesis. Leave out the wholesale "constitutive" role of mind for "experience in general," and stick to its organic function in taking the initiative in the experimental method of procedure, and the philosophy of Kant, too, becomes a superb lesson in enlightened empiricism.[46]

We return to pick up that keen surmise of Hume mentioned earlier—of the naturalistic view of the relation of thought and reality. Hume had suggested that the constant and regular order of our experience on

[46] The significant relations as well as the distinction between Kant and Dewey are well indicated in C. I. Lewis's *Mind and the World Order*.

which we rely so confidently is grounded in "Nature." Kant had earlier reversed the view that man's thinking is true insofar as it conforms to reality, proposing instead that we can have true knowledge only because all phenomena of nature must conform to our categories of knowledge. But a third view is possible, where both claims may be true concurrently and without assigning a priority to one or the other factor. Why not this new hypothesis that the rapport of knowledge and reality comes about through working, so to speak, from both sides, through living, growing, progressive interactions of mind and the natural phenomena of the world? Hume had ventured this hypothesis in his *Dialogues Concerning Natural Religion,* but he had done so without benefit of the scientific theory of evolution which came one hundred years later. Our next subject is the lesson for the new empiricism which was derived from the facts and theory of evolution.

The theory of evolution was a theory of life and it maintained that the forms are not fixed and eternal but have evolved. Each species of living organism has an origin in changes or variations. To be at all, to be born and survive and reproduce their kind, living beings must in every case adapt or be adapted to the particular circumstances of their existence. There is very much that is merely contingent in such a situation. Accident determines very considerably the possibilities of survival, but these accidental factors can nonetheless be ascertained by research. There is, however, an internal factor which Lamarck had pressed into service—the drive of life itself. This initiative is peculiar to every variety of being. As William James had expressed it, a purposive way is characteristic of all organisms and important for their fitness to endure. In general, as Dewey came to see it, the specific forms that endure are always the resultants of vital "interaction" of the creature with other things within the physical order of nature. Every character, every way of behaving, every structure, organ, equipment typical of a species is explicable by reference to its necessary function in the parsimonious economy of existence. "Mind" itself is not to be understood apart from its function in the "vicissitudes" of the life-process. Applied to man as a living organism this means that knowing, thinking, the operations of intelligence, have an instrumental origin and function. They are valuable for life through an intimate connection with action among the interactions of all that exists in Nature. Hence follows the pragmatic view of knowledge. The role of knowledge in a precarious world of time and change and accident is practical. The understanding must concern itself with the passage of events and things as they bear on the present predicaments of men in the particular circumstances in which they find themselves. These circumstances are seen to be no less social, even cultural, than the obvious, physical ones. In any case, the truth for such a circumstanced being is what is found by one's own active efforts to cope with the problems of life wherever they crop up in any region of experience. Even "meaning" itself, Dewey says, repeating his theme of the *Reflex Arc Concept*, is a "property of behavior" or what will eventuate in future consequences.[47]

[47] *Experience and Nature*, p. 179.

"Experience is aligned with the life process," [48] and activity is of its vital essence. Complexity, too—since the process of experience, like that of life, is always one of interaction. Ends are involved, too, for there is a certain teleology of life, but the ends are not *a priori* for they must be discovered through actual trial in the particular conditions of time, place, and circumstance. Always there is the occasion for action and thought, the "problem" which elicits the concern for "the maintenance of a unified experience." [49]

The "experimental" way, then, is envisaged throughout all living nature. Man's own procedure in experimenting is a very special, deliberate, and intelligent mode of doing the naturally experimental business of life. Thus the experimental method is not simply a method of knowledge, but the method proper to all natural existence which knowledge itself only serves.

Within this naturalistic world view the various important lessons for the new empiricism are all incorporated and related to one another, no longer a collection of essays, but the achievement of a whole and progressing philosophy.

The "natural existence" of man—is that the limit of experience? Is our conception of human life cribbed and confined within an image of the biological arena of struggle? And all that stressing of action and the practical, is it not, perhaps, prejudicial to a quiet ap-

[48] *Reconstruction in Philosophy,* p. 90.
[49] *Essays in Experimental Logic,* p. 136.

preciation of the quality of knowledge as a rewarding experience in itself, and to other spiritual values?

Before we let these familiar criticisms gain full head we should reflect ourselves on Dewey's commitment to philosophy as "vision, imagination, reflection." We should remember the manner, too, in which he practiced the experimental method. "A whole philosophy" was our phrase, and it is we who must be cleared, not Dewey. To explain then: A philosophy can be "whole" —that is, coherent, systematic—and gather into one view or insight the things of greatest importance to man, and still not be actually complete in the sense of being finished and done. Time and change, the vicissitudes of existence, are not bounded *a priori* by any organization of thought. The problems that come as they list will always require some new reconstruction of experience and consequently lead to a reconstruction of the philosophy that has previously been interpreting experience. In the terms of Dewey's own thinking and practice, then, the so-called naturalism in which the lessons of empiricism are integrated into one philosophy cannot consistently limit the inquiring or experimental spirit. And the point of this lecture is that Dewey is first and last an empiricist, in attitude and performance as well as theory. Keeping this in mind will guard against other serious misconstructions of his thought.

The scope and adequacy of a philosophy must be judged by the sensitiveness of its author to the abiding major interests and concerns of mankind. We should recall those earliest humanistic interests of Dewey—the concern for the moral being of man, for individual liberty, and for social responsibility—as well as the years of labor dedicated to education in relation to democracy by active participation in the sense of speaking freely and judicially on matters of public importance in national and international politics. Barring all deference to the spirit of intolerance and authoritarian orthodoxy, he was still sensible of the deep human significance of "a common faith."

This man was a true philosopher in his own style. We have said earlier that the challenging predicaments of men (his favorite term was "problems") are "no less social, even cultural, than the obvious, physical ones." The experimental procedure is appropriate for all the varied phases of man's life in society as well as in the world of belief and imagination, wherever matters become "problematic." The principle of the reflex-arc circuit applies throughout this whole wide gamut of experience. The lesson everywhere is that only as men *try* things—for instance, in politics or in art or education—can they really learn to know both themselves as persons and the things of the wide unbounded world that truly concern them.

We must close our discourse on this richly empirical, experimental philosophy with some words, indeed the last words from the close of the *Quest for Certainty*, which surely pertain to our own condition and need today: "The need for large and generous ideas in the direction of life was never more urgent than in the confusion of tongues that characterize present life." [50]

[50] *Op. cit.*, p. 287.

EDUCATION AS SOCIAL PROCESS

By Nathaniel M. Lawrence

PHILOSOPHERS are often accused of being isolated from the concrete world about them. And in some measure the charge is true. However, a proper rejoinder is that although it is true that philosophers are often not much involved in the world, it does not follow that they have but little effect on the world.

The striking thing about John Dewey is that neither the accusation nor its defense applies to him. John Dewey was, from the beginning, *involved* in his world, not isolated from it. And his effects on his world were direct before they were indirect. He is perhaps the only American philosopher to come out of the American foundry with a global monkey wrench in his hand. At Chicago he left his indelible mark on the University of Chicago during a critical period in its history, both as chairman of the philosophy department and as head of the school of education. He also served as a trustee of Hull House. He then removed to Columbia University, where his impact on educational theory is too vast to need mentioning and too diversified to be assessed here. Abroad, Dewey's lectures at the Imperial University of Tokyo had such a stunning effect that even today the academic Japanese visitor to this country usually first wants to talk about John Dewey. Two years of lectures in China were equally successful, and as far away as

Turkey we find Dewey again, this time being asked by the government of that country to draw up a plan for the reorganization of its educational system. The American Association of University Professors, one of whose *raisons d'être* is the maintenance of high professional standards in the face of the United States' constantly expanding need, was organized by a group of men that included Dewey, and he was the organization's first president.

Education in its manifold practice was a lifelong preoccupation with Dewey. And Dewey as a philosopher of educational theory has also been widely discussed, by both friends and enemies, as well as by neutrals. For nearly seventy-five years Dewey's views on education have been the center of a swirl of controversy which has all but obscured the nature of the views themselves. The public confusion has extended all the way from picture magazines to periodicals primarily concerned with ideas. The most prominent symptom of this epidemic of misunderstanding has been the willingness to identify every liberalizing tendency, every radical fancy in education, with John Dewey's philosophy.

I. *The Key Concept: Experience*

The key conception with Dewey, as with so many modern philosophers, is the conception of experience. Dewey as a pragmatist, however, meant something by "experience" which is not to be found in its marketplace usage. "Experience" does not mean merely what happens to an animate being. Experience *is* the fundamental stuff of the world. And "experience" here means events, process, happenings. It is true that the routine business of surviving, securing, and enjoying permits and even demands that we deal with such abstractions as person, thing, time, and place. But in the concrete world about us these abstractions do not float about disconnectedly. For radical empiricism, as James called this position, we do not have just people and things as primary entities to whom purely adventitious things happen. If anything it is the other way around.[1] The backdrop, the substructure, the raw material, or what you will, is the changing process itself. The people and things are discernible strands of identity shifting more slowly, changing less noticeably, preserving a certain individuality and recognizability throughout the world process. However, this preservation of identity, whether it be in the stolidity of the rock or in the spectacular growth and development of the child, arises from within the world process and is derivative from that world process. This is the ancient theme of Heraclitus come to life again, that the world in which we are embedded and from which we arise as temporary constants is a world of endless processive change. It is a world in which the reality of time penetrates to the very root of matter itself. It is the world revealed by the doctrine of evolution, in which species types gradually emerge, enjoy their identity, and either diversify into other species

[1] This theme is too common in Dewey's writings and too obvious to be labored greatly. Its particularization in the field of education is brought out clearly in *Experience and Education* (New York, 1952), pp. 33-35.

or are lost. It is the world of contemporary physics in the analysis of matter, in which inflexible eternal stuff has been replaced by ceaseless electromagnetic activity. It is the world of the anthropologist and the sociologist and the historian, in which cultures come into being by moving stages, rise to a climax of achievement, and become absorbed in an on-going history in which they are partly perpetuated and partly dissolved. It is also the world of the individual self, at least in so far as he is a creature on the *earth*. Nowhere indeed in human experience does the doctrine of change become so evident as in the case of human development itself. It is the task of education to guide this development. If development is lifelong, then education must be lifelong also.

For the pragmatist, then, the world of experience is the final fact, and human experience is but a portion of it. Man arises from nature but does not depart from nature; nature responds to men but does not yield. As it is with man and nature, so in a more intense way it is with man and society. Dewey took with greater seriousness than any man since Aristotle himself Aristotle's dictum that man is a social animal. But for Dewey, society moves forward and changes; society also alters, grows, develops. *The emergence of an individual person within a society is thus the maturing of a process which is itself in the larger process of maturation.* We have here in skeleton the theme which is developed by other lecturers in this series more fully, from which we can not only understand Dewey's assault on the icons of a fixed system of education; we may even be able to sympathize with this attack.

II. *The Old Education and the New*

As we turn to Dewey's educational theory proper we see how central to philosophy as a whole the theory of education is: "If we are willing to conceive education as the process of forming fundamental dispositions, intellectual and emotional, toward nature and fellow men, philosophy may even be defined as *the general theory of education.*" [2]

This passage is crucial in Dewey's writings on education for two reasons. (1) It stresses the notion of process in education. For Dewey, strictly speaking, you cannot *have* an education, and you cannot *get* an education, but you *can* engage in educational activity.[3] (2) In the conception of the "process of forming fundamental dispositions . . . toward nature and fellow men," we find the statement of the theme that education is a social process. These two considerations lead us to ask: "How are the school and society to be related to the profit of both?"

In the first place, the barrier between school and society can hardly be tolerated in the form in which Dewey found it. Secondly, within the school itself the artificial battle between teaching of curricula and teaching of children cannot escape being destructive. It is indeed in the essays called "The Child and the Curriculum" and "School and Society" that Dewey most clearly reveals himself over against his caricaturists, and against caricature to come.

[2] *Democracy and Education,* p. 383, italics Dewey's.
[3] John Dewey, *The Way Out of Educational Confusion* (Cambridge, Mass., 1931), p. 38.

Let us construct, first, a caricature of the "progressive" classroom. The teacher comes in smiling and pleasant, thereby hoping to win the confidence and co-operation of her students. "What shall we do today, children?" she says. When somebody suggests Cops and Robbers, let us say, the teacher gently insinuates the suggestion that perhaps the children should enact one of the great battles. And so it goes with history. When it comes to art, the pattern is the same. Heavy emphasis is placed on the free use of materials, up to and perhaps including the child's garments. If the child wishes to paint some *thing,* instead of just painting, his desire is regarded as a sign of the collapse of his imagination. The unhappy thing about such caricatures is that they are perilously close to portraits of fact. Some so-called progressive schools even now operate in virtually this fashion. But it is a very poor picture of what Dewey stood for in education. It is a caricature of what, at the beginning of this century, was called "the new education." And Dewey regards it as just as dangerous as the old education.[4] He wants no part of one or the other. That is to say, Dewey's own path is *not* a sheer procedural compromise between the "new" education and the "old" education, but rather an effort to embody in principle the best of what each method envisages. The difference is the difference between synthesis and compromise. I quote from Dewey in an essay published in 1902. The passages are sustained and they need to be

---

[4] Dewey never lost his interest in experimental schools, however, some of them definitely of the "new" sort. In 1915 he published with his daughter Evelyn a *descriptive* account of such schools in a book entitled *Schools of Tomorrow* (New York, 1915).

examined with considerable care, for they at once arise from the broader background of his total philosophy and give the lie to those modernists who propose to derive their extremism from him.

Just as, upon the whole, it was the weakness of the "old education" that it made invidious comparisons between the immaturity of the child and the maturity of the adult, regarding the former as something to be got away from as soon as possible and as much as possible; so it is the danger of the "new education" that it regard the child's present powers and interests as something finally significant in themselves. In truth, his learning and achievements are fluid and moving. They change from day to day and from hour to hour.

It will do harm if child-study leave in the popular mind the impression that a child of a given age has a positive equipment of purpose and interests to be cultivated just as they stand. Interests in reality are but attitudes toward possible experiences; they are not achievements; their worth is in the leverage they afford, not in the accomplishment they represent. To take the phenomena presented at a given age as in any way self-explanatory or self-contained is inevitably to result in indulgence and spoiling. Any power, whether of child or adult, is indulged when it is taken on its given and present level in consciousness. Its genuine meaning is in the propulsion it affords toward a higher level. It is just something to do with. Appealing to the interest upon the present plane means excitation; it means playing with a power so as continually to stir it up without directing it toward definite achievement. Continuous initiation, continuous starting of activities that do not arrive, is, for all practical purposes, as bad as the continual repression of initiative in conformity with supposed interests of some more perfect thought or will. It is as if the child were forever tasting and never eating; always having his palate tickled upon the emotional side, but never getting the organic satisfaction that comes only with digestion of food and transformation of it into working power.[5]

If, once more, the "old education" tended to ignore the dynamic quality, the developing force, inherent in the child's present experience, and therefore to assume that direction and control were just matters of arbitrarily putting the child in a given path and compelling him to walk there, the "new education" is in danger of taking the idea of development in altogether too formal and empty a way. The child is expected to "develop" this or that fact or truth out of his own mind. He is told to think out, or work things out for himself, without being supplied any of the environing conditions which are requisite to start and guide thought. . . . It is certainly as futile to expect a child to evolve a universe out of his own mere mind as it is for a philosopher to attempt that task. Development does not mean just getting something out of the mind. It is a development of experience and into experience that is really wanted. And this is impossible save as just that educative medium is provided which will enable the powers and interests that have been selected as valuable to function. They must operate, and how they operate will depend almost entirely upon the stimuli which surround them and the material upon which they exercise themselves. The problem of direction is thus the problem of selecting appropriate stimuli for instincts and impulses which it is desired to employ in the gaining of new experience. What new experiences are desirable, and thus what stimuli are needed, it is impossible to tell except as there is some comprehension of the development which is aimed at; except, in a word, as the adult knowledge is drawn upon as revealing the possible career open to the child.[6]

[5] *The Child and the Curriculum,* published with *The School and Society,* int. by Leonard Carmichael (Chicago, 1956), pp. 15-16.

[6] *Ibid.,* pp. 17-18.

Three themes emerge clearly from these passages. First, the old education is mistaken in regarding the child as something to be cured of his malady of being youthful. Secondly, the new education spoils the child by presuming that his current interests are adequate guides to his future development. It is small wonder that a child so educated, when he comes to college, feels that he has plumbed the final depth of value when he has made up his mind whether or not his courses are interesting. Thirdly, we see that Dewey is aware of the problem which he poses for himself. There must be, he says, "some comprehension of the development which is aimed at." We are here at the threshold of the very concrete problem of the actual organization of what goes into a curriculum, and how its parts are related. The easy old answer is to reiterate a fixed and reliable program, thus abolishing all curricular worries. The easy new answer is to let the interests of the unfolding child take him where they will as he explores the world about him and its broadening horizons. But Dewey finds the former alternative moribund and the latter alternative chaotic. Where then do we go for guidance as to curricular content? Before we proceed further with Dewey's general philosophy of education we must clearly deal with the very pressing matter of what is worth teaching and how it should be taught.

III. *Functional Organization of the Curriculum*

It is the *how* of education that makes all the difference. The great failure of the schools is their failure to recognize that they occupy a central position in a grow-

ing, developing, evolving society. The school is thus
faced with two problems of growth: first the continued
growth of the society itself, and secondly, the growth
of the child who must grow into this growing society.
The problem of how to teach then becomes the problem of how to direct the child's natural growth toward
a functional understanding of his world. Dewey gives
many examples of what he means by useful knowledge.
He tells of the difficulty he had in finding suitable desks
and chairs for the University of Chicago Elementary
School. Finally one dealer put his finger on the problem. He said he was afraid he didn't have what Dewey
wanted. "You want something at which the children
may work," said the dealer. "These are all for listen-
ing." [7] Dewey cites this incident as incisive, a case where
his point was made for him. Learning is an activity, not
a passivity, neither before the spoken word nor before
the printed word. Activity does not always mean pro-
ductivity nor necessarily even participative experience,
but it does mean that without relevance to actual life
the study fails. In the case of arithmetic exercise books,
problems of compound business partnerships continued
unabated long after that primitive method of raising
capital had been replaced by the joint stock company.
Again, gain and loss calculations that have long been
exiled from bank computations live on in the unchang-
ing arithmetic books. And if their usefulness is challenged, the doubter is told that the examples provide
fine cases of "mental discipline." [8] Dewey is no op-
ponent of discipline, but he is too shrewd to suppose

[7] *School and Society,* p. 31.
[8] *Ibid.,* p. 77.

that discipline for its own sake can recommend itself to a young child and too wise to suppose that discipline for its own sake can be educationally effective. Opportunities for relevant arithmetic abound. The problem, says Dewey, is one of "keeping alive the ordinary bonds of relation." [9]

In human society every kind of endeavor is related to every other. No human achievement is independent; no human effort is isolated. The task of the educational process is to lead the young child by developing stages into the main current of the social process. In the social process as a whole, the various fields of human activity have the most profound joint relevance for each other. Any educational procedure which fails to expose the child in a simplified fashion to the ways in which various types of human activity and achievement are mutually involved fails utterly in failing in this.

> A society [says Dewey] is a number of people held together because they are working along common lines, in a common spirit, and with reference to common aims. . . . The radical reason that the present school cannot organize itself as a material social unit is because just this element of common and productive activity is absent.[10]

Considerations of this sort lead Dewey to a strikingly clear-cut pronouncement. "The unity of all the sciences," he says, "is found in geography. The significance of geography is that it presents the earth as the home of the occupations of men. The world without its relationship to human activity is less than a world." [11]

[9] *Ibid.*, p. 76.
[10] *Ibid.*, p. 14.
[11] *Ibid.*, p. 18.

Dewey's conception of the role of geography is only partially exemplified in the contemporary social studies offerings throughout the United States. Let us look at how this conviction was actually put into effect in the University of Chicago Elementary School in the late 1890's.

In this school before the turn of the century a visitor would have found boys and girls of ten to twelve engaged in sewing, in spinning, and in weaving. He might have found some actually engaged in making a loom, others in fashioning a carding tool for combing the wool fibers that were to be spun. Such a visitor would have been a little startled to find that most of the invention in these activities was not imitative but had actually been worked out by the children themselves with only minimal suggestions from their teacher. He would have been appalled, I should think, to find that one group of children spent half an hour in getting less than one ounce of cotton free from its seed, while another group was being vastly more effective in the separation of fibers of wool. The children thus learned that cotton is a luxury of either a technical or a slave society, whereas wool is the common staple of do-it-yourself social units. No doubt the visitor would have felt appalled at the loss of half an hour on so small an insight. He might, however, have had second thoughts after a second glance. He would have found children so engrossed in the learning process that it was difficult to persuade them to go home. He would have found children who carried on their learning at home, self-propelled by the interest thus aroused. What is equally important, he would have found, on a longer stay, the same children engrossed in the elementary physics required for the machinery of production and the functional arithmetic employed both in the estimate of productive efficiency and in the making of tools. He would have found the cultural history of the race exposed to them by way of this point of contact. Not only this, but via this historical route they would be given an insight into those social requisites which underlie the modern intensively industrial society. As we look at this idyllic scene our minds are crowded with doubts: where will you find the money for such an extravagant type of education, even if the time invested turns out to be worth it? My guess is that Dewey would have answered that anything human beings want badly enough they will pay for. We pay rather highly, for instance, for the privilege of putting slum conditions out of our minds. We pay rather highly for the suppression, control, and remedying of juvenile delinquency. We pay, in fact, not only in dollars but in people. We pay rather highly for entertainment whose sole aim is amusement.

There is another class of objection which must be met. I can also imagine an objector, even a kindly-disposed one, asking where shall we find these humanely, rather than merely mechanically, trained men and women whose perspective will be broad enough to enable them to function as teachers of such groups? It must be confessed that Dewey was as responsible as any man for the emphasis on teaching methods. But there is little justification for laying at his door the current proliferation of courses with titles like "The teaching of team sports at the elementary level in decentralized school districts." On the contrary, there seems to be little evidence that Dewey was the least bit interested in pushing subject matter out of colleges designed primarily to train teachers, for the sake of introducing methods courses. The development of further specializations by teachers of teachers in courses about courses represents a fine case of that abstractness which Dewey felt was the dry death for education. Lest there be any doubt about this, let us consider a sustained citation from Dewey which directly bears on this point, namely the point of subject matter over method:

> As against such a view, the subject-matter of science and history and art serves to reveal the real child to us. We do not know the meaning either of his tendencies or of his performances, excepting as we take them as germinating seed, or opening bud, of some fruit to be borne. The whole world of visual nature is all too small an answer to the problem of the meaning of the child's instinct for light and form. The entire science of physics is none too much to interpret adequately to us what is involved in some simple demand of the child for explanation of some casual change that has attracted his attention. The art of Raphael or of Corot is none too much to enable us to value the impulses stirring in the child when he draws and daubs.[12]

I take it that this passage insists upon the primacy of subject matter, that it insists at the very least that method is empy without indeed rather unusual knowledge of the subject matter. Nearly twenty years after the passage just cited, Dewey came to consider the questions of method and subject matter as possible opponents. As might be supposed, he there refuses to regard method and subject matter as antithetical to one

12 *The Child and the Curriculum,* p. 16.

another. Indeed he insists on their commonality. He shows, however, that where methods become autonomous the claim may be made that "an alleged science of methods of the mind in learning, is futile;—a mere screen for concealing the necessity a teacher is under to have profound and accurate acquaintance of the subject at hand." [13]

Dewey subsequently develops the theme [14] that there is no such thing as method apart from highly competent acquaintance with subject matter, and, moreover, competence in the subject matter requires a knowledge of its relations to *other* subject matters in the still broader area of human inquiry in general.

Throughout Dewey's educational philosophy the heavy emphasis is on the contextual status of all intellectual disciplines. The presupposition of any emphasis on method is thus not only a thorough grounding in the subject matter, but also a wide acquaintance with the related subject matters which are as vital to it as it is to them. There should be little doubt that a teacher, perhaps more than an ordinary graduate, needs a broadly humane curriculum in his own educational background. Accordingly, he may be able to spend comparatively little academic time on group projects concerned with the psychological displacement resulting from teaching left-handed children to play the slide trombone.

There may be justification for the turning out of teachers who are long on professional method courses and short on understanding their subject and the hu-

[13] *Democracy and Education,* p. 94.
[14] *Ibid.,* ch. 13.

mane setting in which it lives. But such arguments will receive little support from John Dewey.

We return to the question: Where can we find teachers who have the broad knowledge that will enable them to exhibit the educational enterprise as the interrelation of many disciplines? The answer is that no such teachers are to be found unless they are first broadly educated themselves. The alternative is perfectly clear. The teacher should be reliably in control of his subject at all times. This axiom is accepted by any theory of education. Further, suppose him to be well trained in his major field and equipped with a satchel of methods.[15] He will stick to his subject; he will drill his students; he will demand and likely get a certain kind of performance. His students can participate little in what he is doing. It is best for them to follow him as well as they can. A child's interest is little curbed by curricular division, and the narrowly trained teacher, with his primary need for control, may be unable to judge well a child's efforts at relating his study to his general curiosity. The students will thus be in a state of what might be called conjunctive isolation. Their only real community is through the teacher at the head of the room. There will be no *natural* lines of communication among the students themselves.

From the teacher's being confined to a single-channel operation in his effort to reach the student, a curious result emerges: the students are driven apart. The value of the social discipline present in enterprises like the

[15] Dewey is particularly effective in the critique of artificial stimulation of interest; e.g., *The Child and the Curriculum*, pp. 24 ff.

joint study of cotton and wool which we have just been considering cannot be overestimated. Dewey points out that on the *playground* there is a spontaneous appearance of social organization, division of labor, selection of leaders, and so on, but that in the standard classroom the emphasis is all on isolation, competition, and selfishness.[16] Dewey makes a fine point here, I think. He is saying in effect that at least some cheating is the environmental corruption of an impulse, namely the impulse toward joint effort, which the educational system has failed to harness. Speaking generally, one is tempted to suggest in passing that while school authorities quite rightly look to the home for sources of maladjustment, they might be equally interested in the social function of elementary pedagogy. For instance, the commonplace that children of immigrants speak with no accent should warn us of the overwhelming importance of a child's extra-domestic activities.

IV. *The Root Problem: Corporate Society and Individual Freedom*

Before returning to theory generally, let us take two terms normally associated with Dewey's philosophy of education and reinterpret them in the light of what has gone before. Take "progressive education." This term has long had a connotation of faddism, of pedagogy which was either avant-garde or even *recherché*. There is some reason that it should have such connotation, for surely what Dewey had to say was novel, and the line between what is novel and what is a fad is often

[16] *School and Society*, pp. 14-16.

thin. Suppose, for instance, our visitor to the University of Chicago School to be a sixty-year-old schoolmaster from a small New England town. He will have to stay and watch much longer than he cares to before he will begin to get the point. Again, there was, in the wake of the Chicago experiment, a surge of activity by untrained visionaries whose efforts produced comic replicas, accompanied by howls of public laughter and followed by a generation or so of naïvely expressive but undereducated children. Putting aside these failures, and no doubt Dewey's expansive optimism is partly responsible for them, let us see what the term "progressive education" really means. (It means the emphasis on the nonstatic elements in human learning; it means the stringent requirement of education that it prepare the student for a moving situation of social progress. And it means something even a bit deeper, as we shall see in a minute. It means an education of the child in terms of the history of human progress and accomplishment, for the sake of enabling him to be party to that continuing progress, which we hope will emerge from the future. Without this hope, education becomes an indispensable suit of social clothes, or sheer trade-training. That this system of education is itself a progressive development within educational theory is thus only a derivative notion and one of secondary importance.)

Consider another phrase: "learning by doing." This phrase has become so shabby and meaningless that common consent has at last relegated it to infrequent use. What could it mean as bearing on Dewey's educational philosophy? In the example given, I should think that the phrase would be both meaningful and instructive. It is again only derivatively and second-arily that the phrase refers to the acquisition of manual skills by the experimentation of trial and error, fol-lowed by an increment of improvement. "Learning by doing" refers to the process whereby men come to ap-praise themselves of the full force, significance, and sen-sibleness of any theoretic occupation only in so far as they encounter that theory in practice. The point is that the learning is not merely learning how to do some-thing. Animal association we share even with inverte-brates. We are also learning *what* we are doing. Such practice does not of course confine itself to manual manipulation. It refers, for instance, to the superiority of involving students in student government over against simply harping on the principles of democracy. It emphasizes not only laboratory work in the sciences but a close co-ordination of such experimentation with the theory which it exhibits. It means, in abstract state-ment, that there is no value of learning without the learning of the value. And such value is not to be ob-tained by a series of verbal propositions. And it does mean, as we have seen, the social encounter with so-ciety's common knowledge and common achievement. Let us take the situation described a moment before, the one which I called "conjunctive isolation." The stu-dents are sitting together in the classroom, institution-ally isolated from one another except for their common attention to the figure of the teacher before them. Now let us take them in adulthood. Once again they are sitting together and once again they are virtually iso-lated by nonparticipation, except for the fact that they have directed their common attention toward the television screen. The conditioning for this mode of existence was early, thorough, and extremely effective. And such conditioning cannot fail to have statistically significant results. In the early education of the child he is physically near other children, but socially remote from them in that very practice that is supposed to fit him for adulthood. The subject matter is presented as divorced from other subject matters and with very little of its living significance given. In these minimal—and admittedly exaggerated—circumstances there is only one possible source of interest. The clever child can get a better grade, by competitive isolation, than the next child. And this in a subject for which he may have little use, its usefulness having hardly been made apparent to him.

A surprisingly parallel situation holds with the adult. In his living room he has an advertising machine which, when attended to, takes up a great deal of his time making him feel competitive about the possession of things which he has no real reason for wanting. But the adult's childhood teaching has already prepared him to be docile before this kidnaping of his motivation. We should not be surprised that adults so trained and so nourished should care more for prestige, for power, and for possession than for one another as human beings. Dewey puts it this way: "We repeat over and over that man is a social animal, and then confine the significance of this statement to the sphere in which sociality usually seems least evident, politics. The heart of the sociality of man is in education." [17] The mention of politics brings up another point that can only be touched on in

[17] *Reconstruction in Philosophy* (Boston, 1957), p. 185.

passing. Even those who cast a wary eye at mass media of communication are sometimes paradoxically engaged both in the condemning of politics-by-television and in the accepting of education-by-television. We might do well to ask ourselves more precisely about pitfalls and advantages in each one, since both seem certain to stay.

To return to our original question, I suppose the simplest way of talking about learning by doing is to say that it is a question of how strong the practical and social aspects of knowledge must become in a society that threatens to overwhelm individuality entirely. And it is this question of individual and society in a time of increasing social complexity which is the final subject for anyone interested in educational philosophy.

In order to deal with the problem of the conservation of individuality in a complex society we return first to Dewey's conception of experience.

> On the face of it [he says] the various studies, arithmetic, geography, language, botany, etc., are themselves experience—they are that of the race. They embody the cumulative outcome of the efforts, the strivings, and the successes of the human race generation after generation.[18]

This passage exhibits the very stuff of the curriculum itself as the experiences of the race. Let us keep this conception of the experience of a race in the front of our minds when we consider another passage from Dewey:

> . . . Development is a definite process [says Dewey], having its own law which can be fulfilled only when adequate and normal conditions are provided. Really to interpret the child's present crude impulses in counting,

[18] *The Child and the Curriculum,* p. 12.

measuring, and arranging things in rhythmic series involves mathematical scholarship—a knowledge of the mathematical formulae and relations which have, in the history of the race, grown out of just such crude beginnings.[19]

The import of these two passages is very clear. What the child should be doing in school is literally recapitulating the development of his race. Dewey is here taking a familiar biological doctrine and applying it broadly. The human embryo, as it develops, passes through phases of development which echo its evolutionary past. At one stage the human embryo has the gill slits of a fish, at another the tail of a preanthropoid ape. So also with the child in the social process. Birth represents a certain stabilizing—although by no means, completion —of physical development. The main outlines of species type are indicated, so far as the human animal is concerned. The human animal can now pass muster as human, from an anatomical point of view. He has the proper dentition, cranial shape, etc. But a larger question looms.

What is required to make a human animal into a human being? This is the question which education must face. We know, unless we care to confine ourselves to the biological definition of Homo sapiens, that apart from *sociality* there is no human being. And, as Dewey says, "The heart of the sociality of man is in education."

Like the automatic processes of gestation, which yield a human animal, there are automatic processes of education whereby a fair amount of race heritage becomes invested in the developing human being. This is edu-

[19] *Ibid.,* p. 17.

cation in the broad sense. Formal education is the effort to guide this process of inculturation intelligently.[20]

The model of the biological recapitulation of certain anatomical features of anthropoid development was apparently in the forefront of Dewey's mind for a great part of his career, although he rarely mentions it. Fifteen years after the passages cited above, Dewey returns to this theme with a practical question: What of the features of a race's development are proper objects of study? There must be selection of study topic. How do we select?

> The first office of the social organ we call the school is to provide a simplified environment. . . . It establishes a purified medium of action. . . . As a society becomes more enlightened, it realizes that it is responsible *not* to transmit and conserve the whole of its existing achievements, but only such as make for a better future society.[21]

The starting point for all curricula, then, is this, that they sift and simplify those human experiences which have brought men into definite growth and development, and which give evidence of furthering human progress. From these the curriculum takes it cue.

We thus come to an often ignored feature of the claim that it is intelligence which marks men off from other animals. The intelligence that distinguishes men from animals is that peculiarly reflexive intelligence which can take its own race and its own posterity for its object. Human intelligence is not merely quantitatively different from animal intelligence but qualitatively so. It can take account of itself. In the passage

[20] See *Democracy and Education,* p. 3.
[21] *Ibid.,* p. 24; italics Dewey's.

just cited, Dewey is dealing with this fact in his own way. It appears that intelligence must be addressed to what is worth selecting for a curricular program in terms of the betterment of future society. The brightest chimpanzees can do nothing toward furthering chimpanzee development. Human beings *can* do something about the furthering of human development, for human development is not merely a matter of anatomical maturation. The point is that human knowledge is a function of the whole organism which we call society, but human thought, which leads to such knowledge and which depends upon it, rests in concrete individuals.[22]

We have here come to the final problem, the problem of the individual and society. As we have just seen, the knowledge which men have rests collectively in the social organism as a whole. Human understanding is a corporate thing; very little of it is private property. But the thinking that gives rise to human understanding *is* private property, according to Dewey. "The phrase, 'think for oneself' is pleonasm," says Dewey. "Unless one does it for one's self, it isn't thinking. . . . Thinking is as much an individual matter as is digestion of food." [23] This is the point at which Dewey definitely parts company with Hegel, and indeed not only with Hegel but with the whole tradition of German idealism. He is rejecting any conception of a *bewusstsein uberhaupt,* an overarching consciousness, which merely exploits individual human beings in expressing itself.

We may make Dewey's point for him by considering the problem of freedom and responsibility. Nearly two

[22] See, e.g., *Democracy and Education,* pp. 344-45.
[23] *Ibid.,* p. 353.

hundred years ago our forbears enjoyed an unusual luxury, the luxury of identifying freedom with independence. Just as national freedom meant national independence, so individual freedom meant individual independence. Thomas Jefferson's myopic hope for an agrarian economy in which America would become the granary of the world was typical of the spirit of the time. The independent farmer, living in his self-contained economy, was the ideal of the free man.

It is a platitude that material progress has swept away many kinds of independence. In a highly complex society economic independence, social independence, political independence (in the sense of individual political action) have all undergone sharp modification. The question is, can independence of *mind* survive the ever-increasing tendency of human affairs to become more and more interlocked? When we speak of independence of mind, we are speaking of the last stronghold of freedom, but we are not discussing a merely perishing ideal. It is independence of mind which is the source of all other freedoms. This was the theme of John Stuart Mill's *Essay on Liberty,* published in the year of Dewey's birth. And, as the first lecturer in this series has pointed out, it was in this same year that Karl Marx published the *Critique of Political Economy,* a work which insists upon the corporate involvement of men in all material affairs and, what is more important, presupposes that all human affairs, including the loftiest of intellectual insight, can be traced back to the massive impersonal development of the material features of human life.

Dewey thus stands at a critical juncture in human

thought. The glowing ideal is seen in John Stuart Mill's conception of human liberty. But over against this ideal there stand two plain facts which dominate Marxist thinking. The first of these is the increasingly intertwined character of human affairs of all sorts. The second is the enormous influence of the material aspects of civilization upon that same civilization's motivations and its ideas. Such a society seems to have a locomotive momentum of its own, a forward lunge, a terrible pressure which carries it on its way. The giant question is, "How well can this forward lunge be guided?" Dewey's answer is perfectly clear: Not by a populace whose education has directed them toward being passive, compartmentalized, and narrow. Society's present needs will be felt soon enough. The college graduate will slide into his narrow slot, and economic and social pressures will be happy to relieve him of his freedom and with it his sense of responsibility—for a man without freedom is a man without responsibility. And yet a society in which there is little or no responsibility is certainly headed for destruction. This is the paradox of modern society, not only here but abroad: that it demands a degree of abject conformity which, if unchecked, would result in suicide.

But such a struggle between individual and society is not needed. The alleged opposition between society and individual can and must be undermined. It is possible to have a corporate society of free men, provided those men are properly educated. And proper education must include an outline acquaintance with society generally, in history, in occupation, in science, in art, and so on. As Dewey says, "There is no inherent opposition between working with others and working as an individual. On the contrary, certain capacities of an individual are not brought out except under the stimulus of associating with others." [24]

V. *Conclusion*

John Dewey's views on education lent themselves to some fantastic experiments. It is also true that Dewey himself became occasionally uncritically pleased with such adventures because of their experimental vigor.[25] It should not be forgotten that Dewey is probably best regarded as that singularly forceful thinker around whom the forces of revolution in education rallied. Clearly the disillusionment with prevailing educational practice antedated and overextended his influence. As we have seen, he frequently plays the role of arbiter, as in the case of the "new education" vs. the "old education," rather than accepting the presidency of the contemporary group of innovators. The more stable insights of Dewey's educational views may be discerned through the wreckage of some rather flimsy utopias. At the basis of these insights is the conviction that the unexamined curriculum is not worth having. It is not too much to say that through John Dewey American education became self-conscious on a large scale. But the impulse to examine the presuppositions of what one believes or does can hardly be foisted off by one man on a

[24] *Democracy and Education*, p. 353.

[25] *Schools of Tomorrow*, throughout. Even in this work, a fair amount of the import is descriptive, rather than normative. The authors explicitly disavow an "exposition of a new method of school teaching. . . ."

vulnerable population. It is not likely that Dewey suc-
ceeded with modern millions where Socrates failed with
Athens' thousands. The discontent, the sense of progress, the awareness of need were all there. What Dewey
gave this awareness was a depth which saved it from
mere innovation, setting it firmly in a total philosophy
and orienting it specifically toward the problems of a
rapidly changing society whose educational system, like
its students, was still in short pants. It is a mockery to
lay at Dewey's door those excesses which he partially
deterred.

Dewey was a visionary, and secular visionaries tend to
be unduly optimistic. Human perversity, classically
called "original sin" and equally obscurely known as
"neurosis" or "psychosis," was never properly assessed
by Dewey. He seems to have been what James called
"once-born," the dark places of the human soul being
little known to him. To the extent that he knew them
he shared the utilitarian view that they were products
of social conditions which were eradicable. He shared
the shock of two world wars, but his optimism remained
undiminished.[26] Our judgment might find him defec-
tive, I should think, in that he had at his disposal neither the time-tested views of conservative religion nor
their secular equivalent in the Freudian psychology,
when it came to the analysis of human nature. His great
value lies not in what he ignored or denied, but rather
in what he discerned and affirmed.

These affirmations are nevertheless selective and pre-
scriptive: (1) If the child is expected to grow into a still-
developing society, then he must be educated to the or-

[26] *Reconstruction in Philosophy,* especially pp. xxxii ff.

ganized achievements as they are actually related to one another; (2) The education must be participative as well as verbal, because the child will be expected, as an adult, to participate; (3) If the child is expected to be armed and armored against the smothering and isolating complexity of human affairs, then his education must acquaint him with the ways in which the arts and sciences are in living community with each other; (4) If the child is expected, at adulthood, to contribute the critical thinking which always resides in individuals and yet secures the survival and the progress of society as a whole, then he must be placed in those concrete but simplified circumstances which require him to come face to face with the actual value of the disciplines which he studies.

KNOWLEDGE, VALUE, AND FREEDOM

By Richard J. Bernstein

JOHN DEWEY believed that philosophy sustains the
closest connection with the history of culture. It re-
flects the tensions, problems, and aspirations of an
age. But philosophy is not a passive reflex of a civilization, for its function is to clarify the presuppositions,
beliefs, and knowledge of a living culture, to criticize
this material, organize it, test its coherence, and make
explicit its consequences. Philosophy does not have a
merely negative function; it has the perennial task of
envisioning and imaginatively projecting new possibilities and directions. Philosophy as reconstruction must
combine careful analysis with bold speculation.

When a philosopher tells us what philosophy is, or
rather what it ought to be, we must inquire if his own
practice accords with his beliefs. How does Dewey's
theory of knowledge, value, and freedom reflect and re-
shape the concerns of contemporary culture?

In discussions of Dewey, there has been a temptation
to stress what is unique and distinctively American in
his philosophy, while ignoring the continuity of his
thinking with the philosophic tradition. Unfortunately,
this has resulted in a myopic view of Dewey. We can
best understand the specific problem which most concerned Dewey if we step back and look at him in philosophic perspective.

Though at times Dewey was sharply critical of the

Greek philosophers, he felt a strong affinity with them. He admired Plato for his belief that social and political life could be informed with reason and because his "highest flight of metaphysics always terminated with a social and practical turn." [1] As for Aristotle, Dewey favored his robust empiricism, which portrayed more authentically the world in which we act, suffer, and enjoy than do modern empirical philosophies with their highly artificial and emasculated accounts of experience as consisting of discrete, disconnected sense data. Dewey also viewed Aristotle as formulating a logic of actual inquiry rather than a formal calculus. He considered his own instrumental logic to be in the spirit of Aristotle's *Organon,* but because the nature of inquiry had radically changed since Aristotle's time as a result of the rise of experimental science, so the logic of inquiry, too, had to change.[2]

But what most impressed Dewey about the Greeks was their enlightened naturalism, their appreciation of man as a genuine part of the natural world, where his moral and political concerns are not an intrusion into nature, but continuous with it, and their belief that theoretical knowledge is the source of intelligent moral activity.

The history of modern philosophy, as Dewey viewed it, has been one of radical dualisms and cleavages: metaphysical, epistemological, and ethical. Important distinctions such as mind-body, subject-object, individ-

[1] "From Absolutism to Experimentalism," in *Contemporary American Philosophy* (New York, 1930), II, 21.

[2] See "An Added Note as to the 'Practical,'" in *Essays in Experimental Logic* (Chicago, 1916), p. 333.

ual-social have been mistakenly hypostatized into independent ontological entities. So entrenched have these dualisms become in our thinking, that philosophers have not been able to get man back into the natural and social world in which he finds himself. These prevailing cleavages have not been restricted to the problems of professional philosophers. They have had their most serious effect on the moral and social thinking of all men. In 1920 Dewey wrote that "the greatest dualism which now weighs humanity down [is] the split between the material, the mechanical, the scientific, and the moral and the ideal. . . ." [3] For Dewey this split was the source of the most serious and fundamental problems of our age. He sought to overcome it, to re-establish the continuity between knowledge and value, an ideal which had been esteemed by the Greeks. To accomplish this task, there was no question of a return, but rather a reconstruction of the fundamental concepts of philosophy.

What exactly is meant by the continuity of knowledge and value, and how is it to be achieved? To answer this question, we must first look at Dewey's theory of inquiry. Dewey was provoked into formulating a theory of inquiry by the disparity between the characterization of knowledge by epistemologists and the actual process of gaining knowledge in the experimental sciences. The mark of true knowledge was supposed to be its absolute certainty, yet what is distinctive about scientific knowledge is its hypothetical character. Philosophers had argued that there is a fundamental difference between knowing and acting, yet experimentation—the

[3] *Reconstruction in Philosophy* (New York, 1920), p. 173.

heart of scientific *knowing*—is a form of deliberate *activity*. Traditional empiricists had emphasized the origin of ideas as a test of their meaningfulness and validity, while the important issue in evaluating a scientific concept is its function and consequences. Something was clearly wrong, and Dewey sought to formulate a theory of inquiry which would reflect the ways in which we do gain reliable knowledge and at the same time uncover the errors of traditional epistemology.

I. *The Structure of Inquiry*

Inquiry is characterized as the "controlled or directed transformation of an indeterminate situation into one that is so determinate in its constituent distinctions and relations as to convert the elements of the original situation into a unified whole." [4] It can be analyzed into the following stages or logical moments: the felt difficulty which arises from some conflict or discrepancy within our experience; clarification and careful analysis of the specific problem to be solved; suggestion or hypothesis of possible solutions; reasoning about the logical consequences of the proposed hypotheses; and final testing and evaluation of the hypotheses, which ideally culminates in a resolved and determinate situation.[5] The theory of inquiry consists of the explication of each of these moments, the study of their interrelations, and analysis of their significance.

There are a number of points which need clarifica-

[4] *Logic: The Theory of Inquiry* (New York, 1938), p. 104.
[5] For a more detailed analysis of the pattern of inquiry see *Logic: The Theory of Inquiry*, ch. VI.

tion in order to eliminate confusions and to understand the general import of the theory of inquiry. First, the stages or moments of inquiry are not intended to represent a chronological sequence of what actually occurs in an inquiry. Several of the stages may be merged in a single step, or they may interact with each other. It is not even essential for inquiry to begin with a problem, for we may deliberately reason and experiment in order to discover new problems.[6] Dewey does not believe that men think only when they must. Man is active and experimental. The mark of a scientific intelligence is its deliberate search for new problems.

Secondly, the consequences which are so important for testing and evaluating ideas are not limited to practical consequences: they may be aesthetic, moral, or religious. Dewey's theory of experience is far richer than those accounts that have stripped experience of its qualitative fullness. The preoccupation of philosophers with epistemological problems has led them to concentrate on the aspect of experience which is important for knowing, and to ignore the aesthetic and affective dimensions of experience. There are pervading qualities of experience which cannot be eliminated or reduced to a single type of experience without doing violence to the variety and richness of experience. Consequently, there are also different types or modes of inquiry.

Thirdly, the analysis of inquiry does not purport to be a description of the way in which we always think. Just the opposite. Frequently we are muddled in stating the problem, deficient in imagining possible solutions,

[6] See "An Analysis of Reflective Thought," *Journal of Philosophy,* XIX (1922), 29-38.

and careless and prejudiced in our reasoning and evaluation of hypotheses. The rules for conducting inquiry are normative or regulative, but they are norms which are *abducted* from the ways in which we actually gain reliable knowledge. The standard objection that in order to evaluate the methods of knowing we must first have a prior standard of evaluation is a misleading half-truth. In òur dealings with the world we gradually learn the best means of gaining and justifying knowledge. Eventually rules are learned and explicated. They serve as leading principles for directing further inquiries, and as such are functionally *a priori,* though they may be modified and refined in the light of the consequences of these inquiries. There is a type of circularity here, but it is not a vicious circularity. The process may be more aptly described as a spiral in which leading principles guide inquiry and are in turn refined by this inquiry. There is no mystery here; this is the way in which all scientific knowledge progresses.

Fourthly, the life blood of inquiry consists of rules and leading principles which become funded in the shared experience of the community of inquirers. We cannot conduct successful inquiry simply by knowing the rules listed in a book, just as we cannot become expert chess players by knowing all the rules of the game. We must know how to use the rules, how to employ them in concrete situations. Inquiry is an art which requires careful and deliberate training. It is similar to the fine arts in so far as sensitivity to different situations and the capacity to imagine new possibilities are essential. As in the arts, the rules of inquiry must become the dispositions of the individual. This can only become fully effective insofar as the rules of inquiry are transmitted and refined in and through the informed community.

Fifthly, knowledge consists of the end products of inquiries; knowledge is that which is warranted or justified through inquiry. It has been objected that Dewey has concentrated on *how* we gain knowledge rather than on the *character* of the knowledge gained. But the plausibility of this objection vanishes when we realize that what characterizes knowledge and differentiates it from fancy is not any intrinsic feature, but precisely the method for validating it in inquiry. The mark of knowledge is its warranted assertability in inquiry, not its intrinsic certitude. Furthermore, there is an implicit reference to the future in all knowledge, for future consequences clarify and may necessitate a revision of our knowledge; they may show that what was once taken as warranted is no longer justified. Some critics have thought that this entails the paradox that we can never really know anything, since we cannot foresee all the future consequences, and therefore cannot be absolutely sure that what is now taken to be knowledge is really warranted. This criticism is based on an equivocation, for it assumes that the mark of true knowledge is its absolute certainty, the very point that Dewey denies. But if there is always the possibility of error and logical fallibility, then isn't this a doctrine of skepticism? Again the answer must be no, if by skepticism we mean the doctrine that we can never really know anything. Dewey is not suggesting that we are forever cut off from knowing reality. As our knowledge advances, we progressively improve our knowledge of the world. The doctrine of fallibilism which Dewey had learned from Charles Sanders Peirce does not lead to despairing skepticism, but to the imperative that we must continually submit our knowledge to public test and actively explore its consequences in new contexts, for this is the only way of furthering our knowledge.

II. *The Continuity of Knowledge and Value*

How does this account of knowledge and inquiry shed light on the nature of value and moral activity? How does it help us to bridge the chasm between science and ethics? In order to meet this issue, let us recall something of the intellectual ferment of the latter part of the nineteenth century, when Dewey's ideas were taking shape. This was a time when the horizons of science were rapidly being broadened. Barriers which were once thought fixed, crumbled, and the sciences dealing with man's psychological, social, and economic life were growing by leaps and bounds. Darwin's influence was not restricted to the theory of evolution. Dewey thought that a more subtle and profound influence of Darwin was that he "conquered the phenomena of life for the principle of transition," [7] and had thrown open the doors for the application of scientific method to the study of life, mind, morals, and politics. Today the behavioral and social sciences have become a fixed part of the intellectual scene, but it was only at the end of the nineteenth century that they broke away

[7] "The Influence of Darwinism on Philosophy," *The Influence of Darwin on Philosophy and Other Essays in Contemporary Thought* (New York, 1910), p. 8.

from the realm of pure speculation and became experimental. Dewey, who was not only a sympathetic observer but an active participant in these developments, moving with the crest of this wave of new research, envisioned the reconstruction of the sacred realm of values through the use of scientific procedures. In his enthusiasm, Dewey frequently wrote as if it were possible to develop a science of ethics exactly analogous to other sciences. He has been criticized for his failure to carry out such a program, but this is not what he ultimately intended. Dewey's theory of valuation is important precisely because it is impossible to reduce ethics to a science. We cannot simply deduce ethical norms and values from scientific results, nor are scientific procedures a *sufficient* condition for ascertaining these norms and values. Let us see what Dewey means by valuation, and how it is related to inquiry.

Dewey focuses his attention on the concrete context in which valuation occurs. Man is constantly faced with situations in which there are practical conflicts, where he is forced to make decisions about the course of action he ought to follow. It is idle to speculate whether man ought to make decisions, for the fact is, he cannot escape making decisions. Man does have values, and is a creature subject to obligations. In an actual moral situation the primary question is, What should I do? not What do I mean by "good" or "ought"?—a point which is sometimes neglected by philosophers who are primarily interested in what men say rather than in what they do. The task of a theory of valuation is to clarify the nature of the type of situation in which valuation occurs, and the structure of the process of doing so. It is normative in the same way in which a general theory of inquiry is normative, for from a study of valuation we can elicit standards and guides for the future.

Dewey distinguishes between two fundamental meanings of "to value" in order to explain the context in which valuation occurs. We value something when we take an interest in it, prize it, or esteem it. "To value" in this sense signifies a direct or immediate experience. One *has* values insofar as one cherishes or esteems certain objects or experiences. The other meaning of "to value"—valuation—means to judge, to appraise, to evaluate. It is a deliberative process culminating in a judgment of value. The difference between these two meanings can be illustrated as follows. I may enjoy going to symphonic concerts; this is a type of experience that I prize or directly value. But when I am confronted with the question of whether I ought to go to a concert tonight, a judgment is called for. I must analyze the specific situation, my other obligations, the consequences of going or not going. In deliberating about these factors, I must evaluate the possible courses of action in order to decide what I ought to do.

Valuation is a form of inquiry, and it is analogous to theoretical inquiry. It arises when there is some conflict in our experience. We must attempt to define the exact character of the conflict in order to formulate possible courses of action and to understand and appraise their consequences. There is even an analogue to the verification of a hypothesis, because the actual consequences which follow from a course of action can serve to test the correctness of our judgment. And as in the case of theoretical inquiry, leading principles or rules for conducting practical inquiry are derived from past experience. We can go even further. Theoretical inquiry is *not* morally neutral. We spoke of inquiry as an art which can only be highly developed when certain habits and dispositions are fostered in the individual. He must be sensitive to the uniqueness of different situations, have the patience and persistence carefully to formulate the problem, the creative imagination to envision new possibilities, a bias for objectivity discounting his own prejudices, and the courage to revise his beliefs in the light of new experience. The dispositions and virtues which are required for theoretical inquiry are the virtues that are required for intelligent moral behavior. We seem to be on a two-way lane; if we carefully examine the virtues required for theoretical inquiry, they turn out to be analogous to those required for valuation. And if we look at what philosophers have told us about how we ought to make moral judgments, whether it is Hume with his emphasis on being impartial, or Kant with his emphasis on universality and his warning that we must not make an exception of ourselves, we see that the moral virtues reflect those of theoretical inquiry. But to say that theoretical and practical inquiry and judgments are analogous is not to say that they are identical. Misunderstanding has resulted from a failure to realize that, while Dewey stressed the similarity and continuity of theoretical and practical inquiry, he was also sensitive to the differences.

If we fail to solve a theoretical problem, we may move on to another one, but in a practical situation we are often forced to make a decision. The urgency of a practical situation will also set limits upon the extent to which we can analyze the various factors involved. We are not at liberty to experiment in the same way that we can in theoretical activity, for the action following from our decision may be irrevocable. Scientific information, which in other contexts may be morally neutral, can have crucial moral consequences in the context of a practical situation. Further, the type of conflict which initiates valuation is a conflict in our immediate values. In short, the difference between theoretical and practical judgment is not an intrinsic difference in the process of deliberation, but rather results from the context in which they occur; the pervading quality of a practical situation affects all the constituents of the situation. What does this mean? How does a practical situation color everything that occurs within it? We must take a closer look at the type of situation which Dewey has in mind.

"Sometimes every immediate good or intrinsic good goes back on us," he writes. "We are in the dark as to what we *should* regard with passionate esteem. . . ." We suspect that what we prized unquestioningly is "no longer worth our while, because of some growth on our part or some change in conditions." We may trust to luck for "something to turn up which will afford a new unquestioned object to cherish. . . ." But sometimes we deliberate and "search in order to form an estimate of what would be the good of the situation if we could attain it," though we cannot be absolutely sure that we will prize the object in question "until it has been brought into existence." [8]

[8] "The Object of Valuations," *Journal of Philosophy*, XV (1918), 257.

This description of what Dewey means by a practical situation illuminates the interaction of our direct immediate values and desires, and valuation as a mediated reflective process. Valuation occurs when there is a conflict or perplexity concerning what we directly value, and it is the reflective process in which we decide "what we *should* regard with passionate esteem," what we ought to value. At the completion of an evaluation, our direct values have been reconstituted. In making a value judgment we are not describing the values which we have; we ascribe value to something. We do not discover that something has value in the same way that we might discover that something is yellow, nor do we have a private intuition which tells us that something has the nonempirical property of value. Valuation as reflection "is a process of finding out what we want, what, as we say, we *really* want, and this means the formation of new desire, a new direction of action. In this process, things *get* values—something they did not possess before, although they had their efficiencies." [9]

If ascribing value is not describing what we now prize and esteem or discovering a new hidden property, what is the difference between the values that we have before reflection, and those that we have as a result of deliberation, and how do we decide what ought to be valued? The distinguishing feature of those values and goods which are selected through deliberation is that they are informed or enlightened by our understanding of the specific situation and our foresight of the consequences of the possible courses of action. However, a

[9] "The Logic of Judgments of Practice," *Essays in Experimental Logic,* p. 368.

careful analysis of the situation, and of the consequences of what are live options for us, is a necessary but not a sufficient condition for evaluation. We must employ certain rules which serve as leading or guiding principles in judging what we ought to value and what we ought to do in practical situations. Moral behavior, like scientific inquiry, is rule-regulated behavior. And as in science, rules are learned from, and refined by, inquiry and experience. There is no pat formula for solving moral problems. Each moral situation is unique, and we must pay close attention to the unique and concrete features in order to decide what we ought to do.

But while each moral situation is unique, it is also similar in some respects to other moral situations. We rely on information and principles derived from our past experience. Moral principles become funded in our experience and are the aids for a specific moral evaluation. These principles, like the leading principles of scientific inquiry, are hypothetical in the sense that they may be modified by new experience. They are stable without being static. In a particular situation, they may function as absolutes, as that which is taken as basic for resolving the specific moral problem. There is a sense, then, in which there is an absolute or intrinsic end in every moral decision, but these ends or principles may themselves be subject to investigation and modification in further inquiries.

But now we seem to have raised a new question: What rules ought to govern our moral deliberation? It is not possible to answer this question by listing once and for all a set of rules, just as we cannot list all the rules of theoretical inquiry, for these are continually in a process of development, but we can indicate how these principles are to be determined. We are here on the threshold of answering the question which initiated our inquiry: What exactly is meant by the continuity of knowledge and value, and how is it to be achieved? Before proceeding with our analysis, it will be helpful to become clearer about the direction of our argument.

The analysis of theoretical inquiry has provided us with the clue for understanding the process of evaluation: we discovered that the dispositions which are necessary for performing inquiry have their analogue in valuation. Not that we always exhibit these in making value judgments, for we sometimes escape blindly from moral conflicts, or rely on the dictates of unexamined authority, or follow established conventions, instead of intelligently deliberating about what we ought to do. Just as the analysis of theoretical inquiry is not intended to be a description of how we always think, so the analysis of valuation is not a description of how we always make value judgments, but of how we ought to make them. While noting the similarities between theoretical and practical inquiry, we sought to discover what is unique about valuation, and found that what gives valuation its distinctive quality is the type of situation in which it occurs: one in which there is a conflict of values and desires where we must decide what we ought to desire and do. There is a subjective concern in every moral situation. The function of moral deliberation is not to oppose our desires and direct values, but intelligently to inform them by a careful sensitivity to the specific situation and an understanding of the consequences of the possible courses of action. In this process we must decide what ought to be valued. In asking how this is to be done, we saw the necessity of employing rules or leading principles that have become funded in our experience, for the specific values that are the result of our deliberations are not discovered, but instituted or created in our decisions. The issue that we have now raised is what rules ought to be employed in valuation.

In our discussion of theoretical inquiry, we saw that the leading principles that guide inquiry are continually being developed through inquiry. We also saw that they must become part of the habits and dispositions of the individual, and that this is to be accomplished through the shared experience of the community. This is also true for the leading principles that guide valuation. It is in the community that the very conditions that are essential for intelligent valuation must be nurtured and preserved. And the type of community that can best incorporate the conditions for objective, enlightened valuation is the democratic community. The more inclusive context of valuation is the community of shared standards and norms. Without a stable base, valuation becomes chaotic and narrowly relativistic. But, on the other hand, if there is an uncritical acceptance of standards, then valuation can become blind and routine. It is in the democratic community that the balance between stability and flexibility of common interest can be achieved, where the conditions for free social inquiry, and individual responsibility, can be fostered. This is a plea for social reconstruction, *not* for social conformity, for this democratic community is an end-in-view, an ideal to be realized, not an existent state of affairs. Insofar as valuation is capricious, or follows unquestioned convention, or is hostile to new information, then to this degree we have failed to attain the end-in-view of a democratic community informed by intelligence. At the age of eighty Dewey wrote that "the task of democracy is forever that of creation of a freer and more humane experience in which all share and to which all contribute." [10] The important word here is "task."

We shall be misled if we think that the conditions for intelligent valuation will arise spontaneously, or that they can be elicited simply by telling men to be rational or intelligent. Intelligence is not a special faculty which can be exercised at will. The classic conception of man as a rational animal expresses a pious hope rather than a real fact. Intelligence consists of a set of dispositions which like a tender plant need to be carefully nurtured and cultivated, for otherwise they will wither away. The theory of valuation leads to a program of social action in which we must attempt to actualize those norms and values that will secure more intelligent valuation.

By the continuity of knowledge and value, Dewey does not mean that it is possible to deduce moral imperatives solely from scientific results, but that it is possible to inform our valuations with the same moral virtues and procedures which are required for theoretical inquiry. And, as intelligent theoretical inquiry demands that norms and rules become part of the living

[10] "Creative Democracy—The Task Before Us," reprinted in *Classic American Philosophers,* ed. Max H. Fisch (New York, 1951), p. 394.

fabric of community, so also must standards be shared and critically reviewed in the democratic community to secure intelligent valuation. This continuity does not exist in fact, and it will only be realized through deliberate steps in social reconstruction and education. The continuity of theoretical and practical inquiry represents a task to be performed.

In answer to the classic question, Can virtue be taught? Dewey says that it can, not by imposing a set of fixed values or by transmitting a special type of knowledge, but by encouraging the development of those personal traits which are essential for making intelligent judgments and decisions and creating a community in which fundamental values are shared and critically examined. "Wide sympathy, keen sensitiveness, persistence in the face of the disagreeable, balance of interests enabling us to undertake the work of analysis and decision intelligently, are the distinctively moral traits. . . ." [11]

From this perspective we can see afresh the importance of education, for it is only in the educational process that these traits can be actualized. There is an irony in the recent criticism of Dewey's influence on education, for insofar as our schools have failed to develop tough-minded habits of intelligence, they have suffered from a lack of influence of what is best and most basic in Dewey.

We can also see Dewey's attitude toward tradition in a new perspective. As was indicated in the first lecture, Dewey attacks tradition when it becomes static, that is when it becomes an unquestioned acceptance of

[11] *Reconstruction in Philosophy*, p. 164.

the past and a belief that it is sufficient to answer new problems. But Dewey has also pointed out the futility of moral imperatives unless we take steps to develop the habits, customs, and funded experience that are the medium for effective moral activity. Intelligence is not radically opposed to habit and custom, for these are the instruments for the realization of intelligence. The problem is to keep tradition alive and sensitive to new conditions and to the demands of critical reflection. Such a tradition, in which *logos* reshapes *nomos,* is the backbone of the democratic community.

Thus far we have focused our attention on moral and social values, but we must consider Dewey's theory of aesthetic value and quality in order to balance our interpretation of his philosophy. When Dewey originally discussed theoretical and practical inquiry, he stressed the conflicts within our experience which we seek to overcome. As a result, he created the impression that man is always struggling to overcome an obstacle. The question, with its implicit criticism, was raised: What is the purpose of this striving? Dewey has been accused of glorifying the active life, and of conceiving of man as a technological animal who is always doing and making, preparing for a future that never seems to come. In his later philosophy and especially in *Art as Experience* Dewey deliberately set out to correct this distortion of his theory of experience. Man is not only faced with conflicts to be resolved: he also has consummatory experiences which are the source of what is most valuable in human life. These are vital, integrated, qualitatively coherent experiences. The mark of such experiences is the dominance of a pervading quality which unifies them and sets them off from other experiences. If we think of a memorable experience such as witnessing a performance of *King Lear* or *The Magic Flute,* we can see what Dewey means. If we analyze these experiences, it is possible to discriminate innumerable elements such as the performers, the staging and direction, our attitudes and reaction, and so on. But the experience is not simply a conglomeration of these elements. It has a pervading quality which unifies it and makes it unique. If we ask, How does a quality pervade an object or experience? we can get a clue from the following illustration.

> A painting is said to have quality, or a particular painting to have a Titian or Rembrandt quality. The word thus used most certainly does not refer to any particular line, color or part of the painting. It is something that affects and modifies all the constituents of the picture and all their relations. It is not anything that can be expressed in words, for it is something that must be *had.* Discourse may, however, point out the qualities, lines and relations by means of which pervasive and unifying quality is achieved.[12]

One might suppose that this illustration would occur in the context of a discussion of art, but actually it appears in Dewey's *Logic.* Pervading or aesthetic quality is a characteristic of anything that is distinctively *an* experience. Whether we are creating a work of art, or solving a difficult problem, or making a moral decision, each of these experiences has its own unique pervasive quality. Though these qualities are directly had or felt, it is fallacious to infer that they are only

[12] *Logic: The Theory of Inquiry,* p. 70.

subjective feelings. Dewey makes a subtle phenomeno-
logical point which has been obscured by the prevalence
of the modern dichotomy between subject and object.
Empirically we experience things as poignant, annoy-
ing, beautiful, harsh, fearful, etc. We do not experience
these qualities as projections of a "subjective" mind on
a colorless "objective" reality.

Scientific inquiry has taught us, however, that if we
want to gain knowledge of nature, we must discount
the unique and concrete qualitative appearance of
things and seek constant laws of change that are not
immediately apparent. The uniqueness of what is directly experienced is something we must get beyond in
order to further inquiry.

If we were to be fascinated with the way that the
sunlight fell on a particular solution and brought out
the richness of its color, and enjoyed this experience
without getting on with our experiment, we might enhance our aesthetic experience, but we certainly would
not learn very much about the chemical nature of the
solution.

Scientific inquiry made a great advance when it was
fully realized that to know nature we must temporarily
turn our eyes away from what is most apparent and insistent in nature. But the philosophy which grew up
around modern science led to intolerable paradoxes.
Accepting the classic principle that what is pre-eminently knowable is pre-eminently real, it took scientific
objects as reality par excellence, and devalued what is
not instrumental for scientific inquiry. Immediate qualities were relegated to the realm of appearance, illusion,
and subjective consciousness, expelled from the de-

terminate realm of objective reality. Consequently, there is the paradox that what is most real for man, in the sense of what he directly values and enjoys, is condemned to unreality. The Greek philosophers, Dewey tells us, fully appreciated the importance of immediate qualities in human life, and did not hesitate to consider them real and natural; their error was that they took qualities to be efficacious in themselves; qualities such as the dry and the wet could be causal agents. It is possible to reconcile the claims and insights of Greek and modern philosophy, and to overcome this bifurcation of nature which splits off our qualitative experience from the rest of nature, in a more adequate theory of experience and nature.

Qualities that are directly experienced are not in competition with the refined objects of science for the title of "reality." The dispute arises only when we ignore the context of inquiry, and confuse what is stable, secure, and instrumental for inquiry with the exclusively real. Scientific inquiry ignores certain aspects of nature and of our experience, because they are not primarily important for the purposes of inquiry. But in other contexts, particularly those of direct appreciation and aesthetic experience, the multifarious concrete qualities of experience are of the utmost importance. It is artistic creation that captures and intensifies the unique qualities of experience that are justifiably disregarded in scientific inquiry.

The pseudo-argument which opposes the reality of these immediate qualities to scientific objects results from a lack of sensitivity to the demands of different contexts. This is one more illustration of what Dewey called the most prevalent fallacy that haunts philosophic thinking—the neglect of the context.

The discussion of aesthetic quality and value is not an afterthought, an artificial appendage to Dewey's main concerns. It is an integral feature of his theory of experience and nature, and thereby places in better perspective all that we have said about knowledge and value. Though Dewey argued for a new theory of inquiry that is modeled on experimental inquiry, he did not commit the fallacy of assuming that what is important for inquiry is all that is to be countenanced as real. To do this is to confuse morals with metaphysics, to assume falsely that what is of value in the context of inquiry is the only mark of reality. An adequate and comprehensive theory of experience must take account of what man personally and directly cherishes and experiences, the qualitative uniqueness of experience that is best expressed in art.

Further, we have said that aesthetic quality and value are not limited to a special type of experience; they can and ought to become features of all experience. Dewey said, "The enemies of the aesthetic are neither the practical nor the intellectual." [13] They are slackness, dissipation, incoherence, and aimless indulgence at one extreme, and, at the other, rigid abstinence, coerced submission, and blind routine. This is true for all experience, including moral and intellectual experience. The crude caricature of instrumentalism as indifferent or hostile to the aesthetic demands of human

[13] *Art as Experience* (New York, 1934), p. 40.

life is shattered when we realize that for Dewey aesthetic quality and value are both a generic trait and a regulative principle for all experience.

III. *Freedom and Intelligence*

We have laid the groundwork, though we have yet to discuss explicitly the third member of our triad: freedom. By turning to it now, we can draw together the various strains of our argument. Philosophers have a partiality for talking about *the* problem of something, such as the problem of time, the problem of individuality, or the problem of freedom, thereby creating the illusion that there is one central problem to be solved. An acquaintance with these discussions reveals that there are a cluster of problems which come under these rubrics, and confusion is sure to result unless they are carefully discriminated.

Discussions of freedom have centered on three foci: choice, action, and reason or intelligence. Though various philosophers have given special emphasis to one or another of these areas, an adequate account of freedom must encompass all of them. Does man have the capacity freely to choose, or is he only deceived in thinking so? If he has this capacity, what precisely is its character? But suppose man can choose: does he have the freedom to act as he chooses, or is he restricted by external obstacles? There is still another issue to confront. Man may have the capacity to choose, and be free from external compulsions, and still be in bondage. He can be a slave of his own passions, caprices, and unconscious desires. Freedom, it has been argued, only becomes effective when man exercises self-control and rationally determines his actions.

Dewey's investigation encompasses all three aspects of freedom: choice, action, and intelligence. To understand the nature of freedom, we must get down to fundamentals, and turn to what Dewey called metaphysics, the descriptive study of the generic traits of existence.

Everything that exists exhibits selective or preferential behavior. Whether an electron or a human being, it reacts positively or negatively in the presence of other things. These "preferences" express the constitution of the particular existence and are evidence of at least a rudimentary individuality in all things. Individuality is more than selective behavior: an individual is a history, an extensive event or series of events, each of which takes into itself something of the past and leads on to the future. In other words, the unique ways of responding to presented conditions are themselves affected by past occurrences. The uniqueness of this historical or temporal development is the essence of individuality.

We must be extremely careful, for terms like "development" and "individuality" are highly emotive, and are frequently used eulogistically, but Dewey is describing a trait which in itself is neutral. Individuality per se is neither good nor bad: the crucial issue for man is what he does with it. Our responses may become so routine and standardized that we virtually lose our "individuality." But individuality can be the source of the novel and the fresh.

Human choice is grounded in this individuality which is exhibited by all existences, for unless we could

uniquely respond to challenges, choice would be impossible. As we move from the level of the inanimate
to that of human life, there is an increased complexity,
variety, and flexibility in this behavior. While the "preferential" behavior of a stone is relatively fixed and
limited, the opposite is true for man.

The distinctive feature of human choice is that man
can anticipate and *deliberately* select among alternative
preferences. He can evaluate future possibilities and
intelligently enlighten his choices, thereby giving direction to his life history. As Dewey phrases it, "In so far
as a variable life-history and intelligent insight and
foresight enter into it, choice signifies a capacity for
deliberately changing preferences." [14] The decisive issue
concerning man's freedom is not whether his choices
have causes—for Dewey insists that they do—but the type
of cause which determines his choices. If we allow ourselves to be pushed and pulled, then for all practical
purposes we have no freedom; but insofar as understanding and foresight enter into our deliberation, then
we become free.

It is at this point that our investigation of freedom
links up with our discussion of knowledge and value.
To be effectively free, man's choices must be intelligently informed. The full meaning of this intelligence,
which includes appreciation of the demands of specific
situations, imagination, disciplined thinking, and especially the acceptance of shared norms and values, has
been indicated in our discussion of theoretical and
practical inquiry. We also noted that this set of disposi-

[14] "Philosophies of Freedom," in *Philosophy and Civilization*
(New York, 1931), p. 276.

tions can only be nurtured through the interaction with the proper objective conditions, which in turn are instituted through deliberate activity. Intelligence and action are mutually dependent. Intelligence is the means for enlarging the scope and effectiveness of our choices through planned action, and the latter is the only means for strengthening intelligence.

This brief sketch of the nature of freedom shows us that problems of choice, intelligence, and action cannot be separated from each other. The analysis of any one of these moments forces us to examine the other two. We also gain a new insight into the status of social philosophy for Dewey. It has been objected that Dewey ignores the metaphysical issues concerning freedom for the sake of specific social and political issues, but that these specific issues cannot be approached satisfactorily unless we first solve the metaphysical problems. Dewey insists that no such artificial division of labor can be maintained. Freedom is a potentiality, and like all potentialities it can only be realized through interaction with the proper objective institutions. If it is to be actualized, then we must assume the responsibility for encouraging the development of those social and political institutions which encourage positive freedom. It is the task of social philosophy to clarify the specific problems in making freedom a concrete reality. The typical pattern of Dewey's dialectical thinking is illustrated here, for there is a movement from metaphysics, the study of the generic traits of existence (in this case the selective behavior of everything that exists), to a concern for the social and political problems of a free community.

It is inevitable that when we attempt to catch something of the sweep of a philosopher's vision, as we have
done here, we must pass over much of the concrete detail and specific analyses of his philosophy. Our goal
has been to clear away some of the obscuring myths
which surround the name of John Dewey and to see
more clearly his objective. We have presented an argument in the sense of the plot rather than a series of steps
in a logical proof. It would be misleading to assume or
to suggest that Dewey has unambiguously filled in all
the pieces. The general criticism may be raised that
though Dewey frequently points us in the right direction, he fails to provide us with a careful map through
the thorny paths of philosophic argument. We can illus-
trate this general criticism with regard to one of the
key themes of our discussion.

In his analysis of both theoretical and practical inquiry Dewey rebelled against the dogma of modern
philosophy that experience teaches us only what is and
never what must be or what ought to be. Philosophers
who have subscribed to this dogma have been driven to
the position that all statements of necessity and obliga-
tion are either pseudo-statements or are validated in
some realm that is independent of experience. Dewey
argued that both these extremes are unsatisfactory and
that norms, both logical and ethical, can be derived
from, and justified by, experience without being reduced to general descriptions of what has occurred in
the past. He also realized that in order to justify this
claim, a richer and more adequate account of experience is needed than those prevalent in modern philosophy. Though Dewey adumbrated this position on

numerous occasions, I suggest that ultimately he did not show exactly *how* norms and rules are to be justified in the continuum of inquiry. Insofar as he did not succeed in this attempt, his analysis of theoretical and practical inquiry is still programmatic. In a sense this is a severe indictment, for philosophy cannot be sustained on promises. But Dewey does succeed in revealing the pitfalls of a narrowly conceived empiricism and a rationalism not rooted in experience, and if he does not squarely answer the question of how norms are to be justified, he certainly does provide us with the necessary guideposts.

We must return to the problem with which we started: the role of philosophy in contemporary civilization. "Conformity" and "alienation" have become the clichés of our time, "conformity" on one side of the Atlantic, and "alienation" on the other. It is now fashionable, and the mark of sophisticated profundity, to decry human reason and to despair at the human condition. But this is an escapist reaction. Dewey perceived long ago that the great danger of a modern technological society is its natural tendency to shape a more passive, mechanical, adaptable creature, who is alienated from the community and from himself. It is naïve to expect that conditions will naturally arise that will be conducive to forming a creative, critical, autonomous individual. Man can become dehumanized. There is nothing in his nature to prevent it. We must continually attempt therefore to make the ideal of freedom and intelligence a concrete reality. We cannot be sure that intelligence will win out in the end, but there is little hope unless we make the conscious effort to create a more enlightened, aesthetically coherent, humane experience. And in this task, philosophy, which has also been a victim, in numerous and subtle ways, of the prevailing despair, can and ought to face up to the challenges and lead the way by clarifying confusion and creatively envisioning new possibilities. Dewey's own words are a fitting conclusion to the argument:

> As far as any plea is implicit in what has been said, it is, then, a plea for casting off of that intellectual timidity which hampers the wings of imagination, a plea for speculative audacity, for more faith in ideas. . . .[15]

[15] "Philosophy and Civilization," in *Philosophy and Civilization,* p. 12.

JOHN DEWEY: PHILOSOPHER OF
EXPERIENCE

By John E. Smith

IN RECONSIDERING Dewey's philosophy during the year that marks the one hundredth anniversary of his birth, we should attempt to do him the only honor which philosophers ought to acknowledge, namely, to consider his ideas as sufficiently important to be the subject of continued interpretation and critical judgment. Philosophers, to be sure, always desire to be understood and to communicate with their contemporaries, but much as they wish to be understood, philosophers would rather have their ideas discussed in a critical yet sympathetic fashion. To attempt this appraisal upon the basis of a clear notion of what a philosopher has wanted to say is the most substantial tribute that can be paid to him. And in carrying on the critical dialogue we will be working toward a clearer understanding of the present and the factors that have made it what it is.

Let it be clear at the outset that in reappraising Dewey's thought we have to do with no minute philosopher. In breadth of interest and range of thought he belongs with the great comprehensive thinkers of the past. And in contrast to many thinkers both in his own time and since, he had a constructive program. Philosophy for him meant more than analysis, even though analysis is an important part of the philosophic enterprise. Dewey's constructive philosophy has too often been lost in polemic discussion. I subscribe to the confession made some years ago by Ernest Hocking in which he said that he began to understand Dewey when he started reading him for enjoyment and not for the purpose of showing that he was all wrong. As Dewey's work shapes up in historical perspective, it assumes a great substantiality. One may disagree and one may correct, but in comparison with philosophy of a wholly technical and professional sort, Dewey's large-minded approach to genuinely philosophic questions places him among philosophers of stature.

I will single out the concepts of evolution and experience for special attention because I want to show how the evolutionary idea—what Dewey called the "biological contribution" to philosophy—shaped both his theory of experience and his general outlook on things. In focusing on the meaning of experience, I want to make clear the manner in which Dewey's broader or reconstructed view formed the basis of a metaphysic of nature and a conception of man's place in the universe. It is especially important that we take notice of the criticism leveled by Dewey against the view of experience bequeathed to us by the British tradition in philosophy from Locke to Bertrand Russell. And in so doing we shall have occasion to remark on the positive resources which are contained in Dewey's broader conception. It will be possible, moreover, to show in what comprehensive fashion Dewey elaborated his ideas into a full-blown metaphysical scheme. With this before us we shall be in a position to put several critical questions aimed at assessing the adequacy of Dewey's philosophy for the present situation.

I. *Evolution*

Should the theory of evolution ever lose its grip upon the scientific mind, it might be rehabilitated almost at one stroke by citing the fact that in 1859 the evolutionary process brought forth both the *Origin of Species* and the philosopher whose ideas were to prove so remarkably well adapted to its main thesis. John Dewey hailed the publication of Darwin's work as "marking an epoch in the development of the natural sciences" [1] and he was not slow in claiming that the prominence given to change over fixity in the theory of evolution was bound "to transform the logic of knowledge, and hence the treatment of morals, politics and religion." [2]

Dewey was stimulated by the idea that the very title of Darwin's work represents an abrupt change and an about face; by long association the term "species" denoted fixed forms in the universe, and the theory that these forms themselves have origins meant, for Dewey, a protest against the past and a vote in favor of change over fixity. The emphasis here placed upon change and its omnipresence is at the heart of Dewey's picture of existence as precarious and perilous, characteristics which drive us at once to a concern about the future.

[1] "The Influence of Darwinism on Philosophy," in *The Influence of Darwin on Philosophy and Other Essays* (New York, 1910), p. 1.

[2] *Ibid.*, p. 2.

Closely connected with the primacy of change is the idea that everything must be understood as *in the making* and not as once and for all *finished* or *made*. If things are in the making, Dewey reasoned, perhaps we ourselves can have a hand in the process.

Change means development and this in turn means a process moving in some direction. A philosophy of change must attend both to the mechanism of individual changes and to the direction which they take. Dewey understood Darwin's theory of organic adaptation through constant variation and the elimination of harmful variations through struggle to mean the directing of attention away from *ultimate* purposes and toward an *intramundane* type of explanation. The general or pervasive character of nature can be understood from within its confines; there is no need to transcend nature. Explanation must become a piecemeal and retail affair focused on specific changes and specific outcomes. Attention and energy should be directed to the specific alone, a prescription as binding upon philosophy as upon the natural sciences. "Philosophy," wrote Dewey, "forswears inquiry after absolute origins and absolute finalities in order to explore specific values and the specific conditions that generate them." This is what I shall call the *dominance of the focal point;* the idea that reflective thought is called forth and fully determined by the occasion of a specific problem so that its whole being consists in the resolution of the focal point or problem that brings it into play.

A constant undercurrent in Dewey's thought is suspicion of speculation directed toward what he called "wholesale" problems. We have, he thought, neither time nor resources for dealing with such questions; the relevance of every idea or inquiry to the focal point is always decisive. Dewey is interested in change only insofar as it has reference to human purposes. He is interested in specific changes because he wants to know how they "serve and defeat concrete purposes." As creatures bounded by an evolving environment and yet seeking to shape it in accord with their own aims of living and of living well, man's concern for changes, he thinks, is directed by the way they view the bearing of these changes upon the issues of life. There is thus an ineradicable teleology in Dewey's conception of things; nature turns out to be a most human affair. For reflective beings the processes of nature are not just there in the form of brute fact; they take on the traits of being harmful or beneficial according as they support life or render its survival precarious. Thus concern for special changes is simultaneous with concern for knowing what their outcomes will be and how they take place, so that we may be able to use such knowledge to anticipate and control the course of events. Concern for anything other than the specific distracts attention from the attack at hand and weakens our effort.

The contribution of Darwinism is the establishing of the primacy of change and the banishing of ultimate origins and finalities; the focus upon specific problems and changes; the discovery of the outcomes of such change for the purpose of inserting ourselves and our knowledge into the stream of things so as to influence the results in accord with human plans and purposes; the shift of interest in philosophy away from wholesale and ultimate questions.

If we are to succeed in a world of struggle we must have a weapon both for defense and attack. For Dewey, experience *is* that weapon and indeed this is exactly what he meant by saying that experience is a method, a way of going about things.

II. *Experience*

It is no secret that modern thought, and not only philosophical thought, has been dominated since the eighteenth century by the appeal to experience. When Locke and other figures of the Enlightenment challenged rationalism in thought and hereditary authority in politics, they did so in large part in the name of experience. Experience became the touchstone of all theories and all claims to knowledge. It was, however, not long before the demands of a critical self-consciousness led to thoroughgoing analyses of the nature of experience, and to inquiry into the grounds of its claim to be the final criterion. In the face of such criticism, the empiricism of Locke and the British school—what Dewey called the classical theory of experience—continued to dominate the philosophical scene. The key to Dewey's metaphysic of nature is to be found in the fact that his own theory of experience represents a thorough criticism and rejection of most of the classical view. This crucial fact and its implications have still not been sufficiently understood.

Dewey's emphasis upon science as *method* and his consequent stress upon the operations required for experimental science have led many to suppose that Dewey's empiricism is the same as that of so-called sci-

entific or logical empiricism. This is an error. Dewey
was an empiricist; this was his repeated claim, but he
was not an empiricist in the sense of the term which
would define and link together in one common tradition the succession of thinkers from William of Occam
through Hume and Mill to Bertrand Russell. This
being the case we are led once again to the topic of
experience and to Dewey's understanding of its nature.

In a paper written late in his life, Dewey wrote:

> For many years I have consistently—and rather persist-
> ently—maintained that the key to a philosophic theory of
> experience must proceed from initially linking it with
> the processes and functions of life as the latter are dis-
> closed in biological science.[3]

No more explicit statement could be given to show the
connection between Dewey's theory of experience and
the biological setting of life. Unless we start with the
conception of an organism interacting or carrying on
transactions with the environment, we shall never understand Dewey's metaphysic of experience.

In an important but not very frequently read essay,
"The Need for a Recovery of Philosophy," Dewey as-
serted: "Experience means primarily not knowledge,
but ways of doing and suffering." [4] From this text we
can grasp the leading idea of the entire theory. Experience is a dynamic or temporal affair which is reciprocal
and constituted by all the modes of intercourse between
a conscious being and the environment, both physical

[3] *The Philosophy of John Dewey,* ed. Schilpp (Evanston, 1939),
p. 530.
[4] "The Need for a Recovery of Philosophy" in *Creative Intelligence,* Dewey *et al.* (New York, 1917), p. 37.

and social. The view here expressed is as important for the negations it implies as for what it positively affirms; it is a criticism of older views as well as a program for the future. It was his aim not only to show the short-comings of the older interpretation, but at the same time to establish the closer relation of his own theory to the actual facts.

When he considered what experience meant for the classical empiricists, Dewey came up with the following five-fold description: first, experience means *knowledge* primarily; secondly, it is a *psychical,* subjective, or mental content; thirdly, it is largely confined to the *present moment,* although it may also be taken as the record of past or finished fact; fourthly, it is all *particular* and without connective tissue between its atomic items; finally, experience stands as a *contrast domain* to thought and it is set over against reason as something other than conceptual thought. We can see in these characterizations the antithesis of his own view at every point.

On the *first* count, experience for Dewey is not exclusively an affair of knowledge, nor should it be understood as if it were exclusively material for science. Knowing is an activity that goes on within experience and is controlled by the conditions of empirical inquiry, but the organism also sustains other relationships with the environment and these equally belong to experience. Since Dewey did not identify knowing with either experience or consciousness, knowing could not be ubiquitous. On the *second* count, experience is not taken as exhausted by what is immediately present to an individual or private mind; the behavioristic drift of

Dewey's philosophy rules out such an interpretation from the start. By contrast Dewey took experience, except on its purely qualitative or aesthetic side, as all *public fact.* And this feature is dictated by the function that experience is to perform. As an instrument or tool for shaping the environment, experience could not be taken as a private affair; control demands a means that shall consist of public, impersonal, and intersubjective content. In *Reconstruction in Philosophy* Dewey even defended the development of a purely mechanical conception of nature as a necessary stage in our becoming aware of the possibilities of controlling nature. As long as natural things were viewed as having their own teleological interiors man was prevented from treating them as objects of control; taking nature as a mechanical system was a necessary stage in the development of instrumentalism.

On the *third* count, Dewey was uneasy over the passivity attributed to experience on the classical view. Experience as merely the passive reception and record of the present datum seemed to him no more than an opportunity lost. The secret of Dewey's instrumentalism lies in his view that the present (and the past also as retained) is not chiefly for observation, but is to be *used* by us in a strategic way; from it we have our only chance to obtain a foothold on the future, which alone counts. Taking experience as merely the record or duplication of present fact would spoil the instrumentalist program; our task is not to conform to the world but to transform it through the renewal of intelligence.

On the *fourth* count, Dewey could not accept what he termed the "particularism" of classical empiricism.

In their programs for clarifying our ideas, Locke, Berkeley, and Hume all sought to trace them back to their appropriate sensory data and thus to establish a one-to-one correlation between terms and impressions or ideas. In so doing they came to regard the ultimate or primitive data of experience as distinct, clear-cut first-person awarenesses that are everlastingly singular in character. Dewey objected to such translation on the grounds that clear-cut sense data are actually the result of reflection and intellectual refinement; his charge is that a "reflected product" is being identified with what is supposed to be experientially primitive. Moreover, Dewey could not accept the atomism implicit in this approach. If experience is composed of atomic data it is deprived of its own connections and transitions; this made it possible for rationalists to reintroduce relations as the peculiar contribution of the mind. It is difficult to be sure how far Dewey's objection here is based on the conviction that the classical view distorts the actual facts and how far he wanted merely to find a way of preventing rationalists from capitalizing on the omissions of sensory empiricism. But whatever the answer to that question may be, he had a further reason for his view and it takes us back again to the biological orientation. In a striking use of scientific theory to support a philosophical thesis, Dewey claimed that the fact of survival in the human species is incompatible with experience as atomistically interpreted. "No living creature," he wrote, "could survive, save by sheer accident, if its experience had no more reach, scope or content, than traditional, particularistic empiricism provides for." [5] Here Dewey joins

[5] *Ibid.*, p. 544.

hands with the advocates of "radical empiricism," the contention that experience is never of isolated singular fact, but contains relations or connective tissue within itself. Survival requires some command of things and this is impossible without knowledge of the extended and temporal working of nature and especially of the network of relations existing between its parts. If experience did not embrace this knowledge and disclose such relations but gave only a report, a sort of mental duplicate of purely present and particular occurrences, it could not serve as the needed instrument for success. The future can neither be anticipated nor controlled by a mere image of the present in the form of discrete, singular data.

On the *fifth* count in Dewey's critique we have a point that refers to all the others. He rejected the idea that experience is a single subject matter—the domain of sense—which is to stand as different in kind from, and in contrast with, thought. For him all statements of the form "Experience is X," where "X" means a single quality, object, or kind of datum, are incorrect. Experience cannot be identified with any of its proper parts and it is no longer the given in contrast with concepts. Dewey's main concern was that experience taken in this way must inevitably exclude inference, the activity of reason. For Dewey's program this exclusion would be disastrous; experience in its main significance is *connected meaning* enabling us to handle processes and their outcomes; if it excludes the connections of inference it must again be reduced to the reception of disjointed singulars. An intelligent being does not merely *react* to the environment, but he is capable of *respond-*

ing to it; mind is the response to the doubtful as such. But response involves both an apprehension of the connections between presently discriminated items and the relations to the past from which they come, no less than to the future in which they issue. All of this involves inference and other activities of thought. In thus making essential to experience the activity of the thinking mind, Dewey proved himself a good Kantian. Unlike Kant, however, Dewey claimed to learn all these things from the biologist; Kant, it might be recalled, though he had himself made actual contributions to natural science, had a higher regard for philosophical reflection.

The answer to the question, What is experience? is given in the form of a complex description of what goes on when an intelligent organism stands in thorough-going interaction with the environment. The result is a vast complex of objects, qualities, events, meanings, or habits which determine some future response. And when experience is controlled by the method of the sciences it yields that knowledge of the workings of things which furnishes us with the power to shape the course of events. Experience has many facets; in the nature of the case it cannot be identified with any *one* sort of thing. It embraces not only science and art, but morality, politics, and religion at the same time. If at times Dewey appears to give to experience a singular or differential meaning by identifying it with a method for control, that is because he shared with William James the belief that method is neutral and does not of itself commit us to special theses about the nature of things. It is difficult to understand what leads anyone to suppose that methods remain free of assumptions and that they invariably enjoy protective neutrality. When someone tells us *how* to obtain something, he is assuming that he knows the general sort of thing he is after and has some idea of where it is to be found. To suppose that one-sidedness and special pleading attaches only to results and conclusions and not to methods has been one of the most cherished fancies of the entire pragmatic tradition.

Before leaving the topic of experience a word is in order concerning the seeming disappearance of the individual experienc*er* on Dewey's view. I shall return to this point later on; here we need but note the impression shared by many that Dewey's dominantly social interpretation of experience as public fact makes it difficult to locate the individual for whom experience is an actual fact. It is true that Dewey sought to deal with this problem by means of the doctrine of pervasive quality and what he called having *an* experience; the aesthetic dimension, it would appear, makes room for the individual and the private. But even in this context Dewey retained his suspicion of the private; emotions, he wrote, "are not, save in pathological instances, private," [6] but are occurrences in the development of experience to some issue or conclusion. This seems to place the most individualized of all experiences once again in the public context where it falls under the dominant motive to control events.

Dewey used with considerable success his doctrine of method for the purpose of establishing continuity between knowing and evaluating in the ethical sense. And this he could achieve because he viewed each as a proc-

[6] *Art as Experience* (New York, 1958), p. 42.

ess aiming at some sort of control. Connecting the scientific and the aesthetic, however, is more difficult because the aesthetic is not supposed to be a matter of instrumentalities at all, but of intrinsic finality. The aesthetic for him must either lose the consummatory value claimed for it, or we must admit a genuine, individualized, final center of experience. Thus our difficulty in locating the individual who has first-person experience stems from the fact that even in the aesthetic dimension Dewey is not always able to avoid slipping back into his thoroughgoing instrumentalism.

We come now to our third theme, Dewey's metaphysics. It is clearly impossible to set forth even a skeleton outline of the substantive position contained in Dewey's most comprehensive metaphysical book, *Experience and Nature*. But we shall nevertheless use it as a guide in the development of our third theme. The persistent neglect of that important book has been largely responsible for the truncated view of Dewey's philosophy that has been entertained no less by his followers than by his avowed critics.

III. *Metaphysics*

Dewey developed his position into a full-blown metaphysical system which he described as naturalistic empiricism. There can be no question that in the final construction of his naturalistic philosophy, Dewey was guided largely by the evolutionary idea and the reconstructed conception of experience. Each determines an aspect of his theory of nature and of his view of man as a creature firmly planted in the natural process.

At the outset of *Experience and Nature* Dewey distinguishes between philosophy and metaphysics; "if we follow classical terminology," he writes, "philosophy is love of wisdom, while metaphysics is cognizance of the generic traits of existence." [7] The upshot of this distinction is that metaphysics should mean the delineation of the most general and pervasive traits exhibited by anything that exists, whereas philosophy is bound up with the basic aims and strategy of life. Existence and individuality, event and relation, function and structure and many other categories become the appropriate concern of metaphysical analysis. Dewey objected vigorously, however, to the idea that the pervasive structure disclosed by analysis is to be set off as a timeless realm more real than the world of contingency and change. He objected, moreover, to metaphysics taken in any sense other than the one he had set out. The aim of metaphysics is to arrive at a structural catalogue; there is to be no synthetic interpretation of things by selecting any one aspect or feature as the clue to the unity of the whole.

He repeatedly maintained that the generic traits of existence are themselves involved in time and change and that man is related to these features of nature in a practical way. This fact shows us that metaphysics is not enough; if man is to succeed and improve his lot in a precarious world he needs what Dewey called the wisdom that is philosophy as well. This latter note is sounded with special force in his final chapter where he returns again to the connections between philosophy and metaphysics. There we see emerging the idea that

[7] *Experience and Nature* (New York, 1929), p. 51.

philosophy is essentially *criticism,* that is, appraisal and judgment directed toward goods or values. The aim of philosophy as criticism is the relating of different aspects of experience to each other and the reflective discovery of genuine or lasting values as distinct from what is trivial or evanescent. It is in this way and at one stroke that Dewey settled accounts with the classical conception of philosophy as love of wisdom and introduced into his system a wisdom that is not knowledge but that cannot be separated from knowledge.[8]

But howsoever we interpret the wisdom that is philosophy, we still need further clarification as to the relation it bears to metaphysics, the relation that is between the wisdom that is to guide life and the pervasive or generic nature of the universe in which it is to be lived. We come here to the heart of Dewey's philosophical vision and it makes no difference by what name we choose to call it. The principal point is that for him there is a vital and practical relation existing between the generic traits of the universe on the one hand and the issues of life and death faced by those who live in it on the other. Dewey described this relationship as raising the "most far-reaching question of all criticism" and as the problem of problems for reflective thought—the relation between existence and value. If, for example, we discover precariousness as a trait of all things, that fact by itself has no more significance than that of a trait noted and recorded. When, however, precariousness is seen as connected with the concrete situations in which men choose, live, and die, it takes on, says Dewey, "that fear of the Lord which is at least the beginning of wis-

[8] *Experience and Nature,* p. 409.

dom." [9] All, then, finally turns on man, the emphasis in Dewey's philosophy which led Santayana to accuse him of natural impiety. To the extent to which natural process affects us or we intervene in natural process, the situation becomes decisively related to values. As if to secure the point more firmly, Dewey writes:

> The more sure one is that the world which encompasses human life is of such and such a character (no matter what his definition), the more one is committed to try to direct the conduct of life, that of others as well as of himself, upon the basis of the character assigned to the world.[10]

If we stand off and try to view Dewey's vast and complex philosophy without regard to the technical apparatus of philosophers, we see an enormous spread of nature, of things and processes, of powers and their effects; these constitute the environment in its nonhuman aspect. And we see man—the being with intelligence in whom the human predicament, as Dewey says, "becomes aware of itself." That is the whole picture, nature and man. There is no third party and indeed man is so completely a part of nature that it often seems as though there were no second party. Nature is an evolving affair, filled with change and marked by precariousness and instability; man has experience, that product of his mind and his transactions with the environment containing within itself both the knowledge born of science and the wisdom of philosophy that is supposed to guide him in its use. Living, then, becomes the grand strategy of seeking to *control* the passage of things so as to make life not only sufficiently stable for survival, but to enhance its quality

[9] *Ibid.*, p. 413.
[10] *Ibid.*, pp. 413-14.

and enjoyment through the cultivation of those lasting goods discovered in experience and approved on reflection. The futurism of Dewey's thought is dictated by this grand strategy; every present has its being as an opportunity for discovering the secrets of things, how they work and where they lead, so that we may gain power over the future. On this reading life is not so much lived as it is taken by storm. There is an experimental spirit and a restlessness hanging over it all, for in the final reach there is no fulfillment in Dewey's universe; one never possesses, but is always on the way to possess. The past is gone, the present is unstable and pregnant with care; besides, the present is but an instrument for the future and the future never comes. For every present is analyzed not in terms of what it *is,* but rather by reference to what it *will do,* and we are once again put off to the future. The point is most clearly illustrated in the case of the knowledge process. Dewey always distinguished between *having* and *knowing,* the former meaning direct, present experience. But if we ask whether *knowledge* is ever *had* as distinct from the having of "an experience of knowing," Dewey would have to answer in the negative. Knowledge is never had, but is always infinitely postponed; what we can have in the present is an hypothesis or theory the meaning and justification of which always lies in the future.

It is impossible to expound or interpret philosophical ideas without giving at least implicit critical judgment, but implicit criticism is not enough; appraisal of a more positive sort is called for. I shall, therefore, focus upon three issues raised by the themes I have set forth. And in considering these criticisms we do well to bear in mind that insofar as Dewey stands as *the* American philosopher for the first half of our century at least, we pass critical judgment upon ourselves.

The first issue concerns whether Dewey was right in his insistent and persistent claim that man must forswear what he called "wholesale" questions in favor of specific or retail problems. How far, in other words, is it valid to admit what I have called the dominance of the focal point. Are the so-called practical and urgently focused predicaments the only human concerns? In considering this question we must begin by admitting that Dewey's aim in emphasizing the specific and piecemeal problem is clear and not without its measure of truth. We have limited resources and limited opportunities for strengthening our hand; much of our energy must be directed toward meeting the immediate challenge of the environment. No effort is to be wasted on inquiries into large "useless" questions such as why there is evil in the world, whether there is God, how one and the same individual can retain identity while still changing from day to day. As far as this goes we may accept his doctrine of the need for intelligent attack upon the evils and threats of the environment. But a major difficulty at once confronts us: how shall we determine what is *relevant* to resolving the piecemeal problem and indeed how shall we know when it is resolved? To what extent are ultimate and apparently useless questions at the heart of a difficulty which seems overwhelmingly specific and practical? No natural science will answer these questions all by itself.

It is not, however, merely a matter of showing the

practical relevance of wholesale or ultimate questions;
this can always be done and Dewey at times acknowl-
edges the point himself when he thinks of reflective
thought as criticism. But more important, ultimate
questions point to our human concern for some understanding about aspects of our life and world beyond the
reach of what is taken into account by a philosophy directed only to the instrumental control of things. The
only point in Dewey's thought where an attempt is
made to transcend the instrumental attitude is in
aesthetics; this is the one aspect of experience that is
offered *for itself* and not as a means to something else.
But we may well ask whether the aesthetic is enough;
there are in addition large questions of a *distinctively
moral* nature that are not the same as choice between
technical alternatives, and there are problems perennial
in metaphysical analysis and speculation, to say nothing
of the concerns of religion. What are we to do in the
face of the persistent human demand—I almost said
natural demand—for answers to such questions as
whether an individual is responsible for a world and a
self he never made, whether human purpose and choice
are but the inner appearance of a supposedly real world
composed only of physical events; what are we to make
of the fact that the universe contains a self-reflexive or
self-representative being in the form of self-consciousness, whether there is self-dependent being? These are
questions which the philosopher cannot avoid, because,
if I may borrow a phrase from Dewey, they belong to
the "problems of men." But they will be ignored, as indeed they were by Dewey, from the standpoint of a phi-

losophy acknowledging only specific problems and the instrumental response.

The second issue is closely related to the foregoing; it concerns the theory of experience and especially whether Dewey's interpretation of it as an instrument and public fact does not mean the disappearance of the individual self or experiencer. In making this criticism I must confess to a certain ambivalence; on the one hand I hold that his account of experience conforms more closely to the facts than does the classical theory. His account, it must be admitted, brings within experience much that is actually encountered but which had to be denied experiential status on the classical view. On the other hand, however, Dewey went so far in the direction of behaviorism or the translation of experience into external, public fact and function that the individual experiencer becomes insignificant. The individual and the private always made Dewey uneasy; it is not that he denied either, he was too good an empiricist for that, but he wanted to keep them confined to a place where they would do no public damage. He intended to provide for the privacy of experience by his theory of art and through what he called the enhancing and enriching of experienced goods. But when it comes to experience as the instrument or weapon of attack on the environment, privacy and individuality are of no account. The fact that an individual self is always the locus of experience, that experience, as William James put it, is always somebody's experience, somewhere and somewhen, is not taken seriously; as either overt behavior or impersonal public fact, experience virtually closes with nature, and the individual is forced to abscond into the realm of art.

It is no accident that Dewey was forced to acknowledge this deficiency in the face of psychological criticism. In reply to Allport's questions concerning his psychology, Dewey candidly replied: "I am obliged to admit what he says about the absence of an adequate theory of personality." [11] And the reason offered by Dewey in his own defense was his desire to avoid "spiritualistic" theories of the self as individual substance. But even if we admit the inadequacy of the concept of substance, surely the problem of locating the unity and identity of the individual self remains. This problem cannot be resolved, as William James's entire philosophical development testifies, by a purely functional theory. Every functional theory of the self ends by translating it into activities of a sort which only a center of consciousness can perform. "I would point out," Dewey wrote in 1939, "that I hold that the word 'subject' if it is to be used at all, has the organism for its proper *designatum*. Hence it refers to an *agency of doing*, not to a knower, mind, consciousness or whatever. . . ." [12] I confess that I fail to follow when I am told that a person is not a consciousness or a knower, but, even more, I fail to understand how an "agency of doing" can become aware of itself, how it can remember and how it can become divided within itself.

How, for example, are we to understand the divided self as an unhealthy or undesirable state of affairs unless we presuppose an underlying unity and center of the

[11] *The Philosophy of John Dewey*, p. 555.
[12] *Ibid.*, p. 542.

self? Dewey could not really introduce such questions into his theoretical treatment because for him all theory is instrumental to further control; if the answer to a given question does not contribute directly to the manipulation of a portion of nature it is of no account. The more a problem relates either to the ultimate constitution of things or to the interior life of an individual self, the further removed it is from the surface of public fact and the less powerful would be its theoretical solution for the control of the environment. But not all human problems are directly a matter of overt and external control of things; some of them have to do with the interpretation of individual life and its purpose. When these "useless" questions are neglected, they do not simply evaporate; on the contrary, they take on an explosive urgency just to the extent to which they are ignored. And if all the available intellectual discipline for treating them is at work elsewhere, we should not be surprised when others seek to resolve the problems confronting the individual, his freedom, his purpose, and his life in the world in what appears as an irrational way. We earn the right to criticize these attempts at solution only when we are seeking to answer the same questions. To refuse to raise a question is to forfeit the right to assess the answers offered by others.

The third and final issue concerns the nature and function of metaphysics itself. Dewey repeatedly rejected what he took to be the main distinction behind classical metaphysics, the distinction between appearance and reality. He was fond of saying that the proper contrast to appearance is not reality but disappearance. The point of his rejection is that no one aspect of things and no one portion of experience can be taken as the clue to or as definitive of the exclusively real so that everything else is reduced to the domain of appearance. Selective preference must be overcome; nothing special or limited can be elevated to an absolute position. Everything must be taken into account and given its due, and the singling out of any one thing or trait as a clue for interpreting all the rest appears as hopeless partiality and special pleading. Now when such a thesis is advanced in the contemporary world it has an undeniable democratic tone which commends it to many; it especially satisfies our interest in remaining neutral in the face of those hard problems which cannot be solved in what appears to be a final or definitive way. But our concern is neither with the overtones of such a view nor with the fact that it satisfies a current interest, but with the question as to whether it is true and most adequately expresses the nature of metaphysics. I believe that it does not and for two main reasons.

First, there is no point whatever in bothering our heads over the general nature of things if the only conclusion at which we shall arrive is one we knew well enough in the beginning, namely, that reality is a quite miscellaneous collection of things related in some fairly constant ways. We scarcely need metaphysical inquiry to achieve that result any more than we would need it to conclude that whatever is, is. Without a differential standpoint or interpretative principle such as organism, matter, or selfhood, from which we attempt to understand reality in its wholeness, we have no insight and ultimately no philosophy. I do not say that the interpreting principle need imply any static monism; I wish only to point out that a radical pluralism will not do as an adequate metaphysical principle because it can never get beyond repeating, in the form of what purports to be a critical conclusion, the fact known to all at the outset, namely that reality contains as many things as it does in fact contain.

Secondly, it is not merely a matter of making a plea for the employment of a differential principle of interpretation in philosophy, but rather of pointing to the unavoidability of such a principle. Hegel, for example, surpassed all philosophers in his attempt to avoid a limited or special vantage point from which to estimate the whole, but if we attend to what actually happens in his system we find that he was actually asking for a special principle rich enough to interpret the whole of reality. This principle in his system is self-consciousness or spirit; on any interpretation what we are given is certainly a differential principle. It is not in fact different with Dewey's own philosophy. For all of his criticism of absolutes and of an ultimate context, Dewey's naturalistic empiricism does not avoid a vantage point from which it interprets reality as a whole. A great deal of the power of Dewey's thought in American life has in fact been due to the circumstance that he did not follow his own prescriptions. Dewey's thought is deeply involved in a differential principle governing the interpretation of the whole of nature and of man's place in it; the biological situation—the interaction of organism and environment plus the mutual adjustment required for survival—furnishes the key to understanding the human predicament; experience in the form of science provides us with the exclusive instrument for coping with it.

Dewey's view of what he called the human predicament is thoroughly dependent upon taking biological theory as the clue to man's place in the universe. Existence changes and is precarious; the environment is not all favorable to the sustained life of man; as a peculiar type of biological organism man is capable of experience or the attainment of public knowledge. When shot through with intelligent method, experience can intervene to control the environment and thus make possible the turning of nature's processes to human ends. This basic vision controlling the whole of Dewey's philosophy is itself totally dependent upon taking one aspect of the full situation of man in the universe and using it as a clue to the nature of the whole. The biological and the social, as Dewey repeatedly stressed, determine his outlook; if they had not he would have produced no philosophy, but only a social theory.

I cannot pass over the problem of selective emphasis without a final word about the most glaring form in which it is raised by Dewey's thought. For Dewey the name for the real is Nature and we are often told by him that no differential meaning should be attached to the term. Nature is all there is and we must not suppose that the concept of nature derives its meaning from the contrast situation in which it stood in the traditional "great chain of being," where it was bounded by man at one end and by God at the other. But if the term "nature" is to have no differential meaning and simply denotes "whatever is," then it is gratuitous. For we encounter persons and poems, tables and chairs, hopes and fears. All are real and stand in need of analysis and interpretation, but exactly what is contributed by using the term "nature" to denote all these different kinds of things? The term "nature" is far from innocent. By it Dewey means to denote the environment including man and perhaps all their potentialities, but nothing more. That nature, however, taken in some differential sense, exhausts reality, Dewey has nowhere shown.

Negative notes need cause no embarrassment on a commemorative occasion. For what better tribute to a distinguished philosopher can one offer than the attempt to think his thoughts after him and thus to become engaged in a critical way with the problems he has faced? We respect most those philosophers we take seriously enough to criticize.